Uncharted Seas

Uncharted Seas

Fuller Albright, M.D.

Read Ellsworth, M.D.

Edited by D. Lynn Loriaux, M.D., Ph.D.

KALMIA PRESS
PORTLAND, OREGON

Grateful acknowledgment is made to the Countway Library for assistance in the publication of this book. Photograph of Fuller Albright courtesy of Read Albright; photographs of Read Ellsworth and Jacob Erdheim courtesy of the National Library of Medicine, History of Medicine Division.

JBK Publishing
Post Office Box 69487
Portland, Oregon 97201

Contents

Editor's Introduction

Fuller Albright was born in Buffalo, New York on January 12, 1900. He was born to opportunity. His father, John Joseph Albright, was a wealthy businessman with interests in coal, asphalt, steel, and automobiles. John's first wife, Harriet, died in 1895, leaving him with three children: Raymond, Ruth, and Langdon. Ruth was sixteen. Her father, believing she needed a woman's influence and guidance, wrote to the president of Smith College seeking a young woman of character and accomplishment who could serve as Ruth's governess. The post was offered to a recent graduate, Susan Fuller, and she accepted. Two years later, John Albright and Susan Fuller were married. They had five children. Fuller, the second of two sons, was the middle child.

Fuller Albright was, from the outset, physically and intellectually robust. He was gifted but not precocious. His father had founded the Nichols School, a private school for boys in Buffalo. Fuller, like other Albright boys before him, attended Nichols. He was a good scholar and captain of the football team. Still, it was not readily apparent that he was destined for a career in clinical science that would prove to be unparalleled for sustained productivity and for novel and profound insight.

Many families of wealth in the early part of this century spent their vacations in elite enclaves. The Jekyl Island Club, off the coast of Georgia, was a favorite of the Albright family. When John Albright desired simplicity, however, he retired to a family retreat on the shores of Wilmurt Lake in the Adirondacks. This was his favorite place, and it soon became the favorite haunt of Fuller as well. It was here that Fuller acquired his lifelong love of fly fishing, developed the woodsman's skills that he treasured, and found a deep-seated reverence for the natural world that would serve to refresh him over and again throughout his life. His attributes of self-reliance and independent thought perhaps derived in large measure from these beginnings. He had a devotion to this place which was incandescent. He spent a month of nearly every summer of his life here. The first codicil of his will details the disposition of his share in the property. He directed that his ashes be scattered here.

Fuller went to Harvard College. With America's entry into the First World War, he falsified his age and joined the army, having been at Harvard only eighteen months. He was sent to Officer Candidate School in Plattsburg, New York. Here, it is likely that a fateful event occurred that would come to dominate the course of his life. This was the time of the great influenza pandemic. The disease ravaged army training camps, and few recruits were spared. Most recovered completely. For some, however, a time bomb of devastating effect was left ticking within: post-encephalitic Parkinson's disease.

The end of the war found Albright an instructor in the Student Army Corps at Princeton University. In spite of having only a year and a half of college work to his credit, he was admitted to Harvard Medical School in 1920. He flourished there, and was elected to the Alpha Omega Alpha medical honor society in 1923. Graduating in 1924, he took an internship at the Massachusetts General Hospital, where he served until 1926. It was during these two years that he met and became friends with Read Ellsworth.

Little is known of Ellsworth. He graduated from Reed College in Portland, Oregon and attended Johns Hopkins Medical School. He was bright (some say brilliant), outgoing, and full of life. When he returned to Johns Hopkins, he lived near the hospital, on Wolf Street. He painted his door red so that people would have no trouble finding him. He contracted pulmonary tuberculosis, which in time proved fatal.

Albright and Ellsworth together came under the spell of Joseph Aub, one of the earliest American clinical scientists in the emerging field of endocrinology and metabolism. Both men determined to follow Aub's example in some way. Albright worked with Aub during the year following his internship. Ellsworth returned to Johns Hopkins where Albright joined him in 1927. They began a fertile collaboration on the physiology and pathophysiology of calcium metabolism that continued until the untimely death of Ellsworth in 1937.

Albright journeyed to Vienna in 1928 to work with the famed pathologist Jacob Erdheim. He would later say of him that, "Quite simply, he knew more about human disease than any other living man." He went to Erdheim with a well-developed scientific mind, but it was Erdheim who recognized and encouraged the expression of Albright's extraordinary powers of intuition and inductive thinking. The beginning of Fuller Albright's career as an independent

Read Ellsworth in his laboratory at Johns Hopkins

scientist can be traced to this association with Erdheim.

Returning to the Massachusetts General Hospital in 1929, Albright established the Biological Laboratory, which offered the Aschheim-Zondek pregnancy test for the hospital. As the repertoire of tests grew, the name was changed to the Endocrine Laboratory. This laboratory subsequently became the core of the world-famed Endocrine Unit of the Massachusetts General Hospital.

Work on *Uncharted Seas* seems to have begun in 1930. In this same year, the wedding of a friend served to introduce Albright to Claire Birge of Greenwich, Connecticut. He courted her, and they were married in 1932. As a wedding gift, her father gave them the money to build the house at 271 Goddard Avenue in Brookline. The Albrights would live in this house for the remainder of Fuller's life. Their first child, a son, was born in 1935. He was named Birge after his mother, as Fuller had been named for his mother before him.

When Albright first suspected that he was developing Parkinson's disease is not precisely known; when it first became apparent to a colleague is. At the annual clinical science meeting in Atlantic City in May of 1936, Fuller and John Eager Howard were sitting in their hotel room rehearsing talks for each other when Fuller suddenly said, "You have been looking at my thumb; do you think that I am getting Parkinson's disease?" Howard had indeed been watching the first signs of the characteristic pill-rolling tremor of the disorder, but he denied the thought. Within a year, however, the signs were unmistakable, and the diagnosis became apparent to everyone.

This blow was followed in rapid succession by the deaths of Read Ellsworth, Albright's closest friend, and Jacob Erdheim, his hero. Work on *Uncharted Seas* appears to

Jacob Erdheim

have ended at this time. A second son was born in 1938. He was named Read Ellsworth Albright.

The disease progressed rapidly. By 1940, Fuller could no longer write. By 1945, his speech was difficult to understand. By 1950, he was convinced that the disease was affecting his intellect. It placed a heavy burden on both his personal and professional life.

It is noteworthy that this disease, characterized by rigidity and lack of spontaneity, can induce these same changes in the life style of those who suffer from it. Albright, with time, settled into a fixed daily, weekly, and yearly schedule. The day started at seven o'clock. Breakfast, "the most important meal of the day," was cereal, eggs, and toast. Before leaving for the hospital, Claire would put lunch money in one jacket pocket, where it could be found by the hospital lunchroom cashier, and several handkerchiefs in the other. Fuller would be driven to work by the third-year medical student currently taking an elective with him. This student would be given full use of the second car in return for this service.

They would arrive at the hospital around nine o'clock and Fuller would spend the early morning at his desk, with correspondence. Rounds were at eleven o'clock. Every patient was seen. After rounds, the group would lunch together and then adjourn to afternoon clinic. There was a stone clinic one day and an ovarian dysfunction clinic on another. One afternoon was devoted to a review of the data collected during the preceding week. This conference continued until all of the data had been seen and discussed. Other afternoons were spent preparing lectures, making slides, and revising manuscripts. The rule was eight versions per paper. (In sharp contrast with our time, only one day a year was devoted to funding. All grant applications would be written on this day. Only on this day would monetary issues be discussed with the staff.)

Albright would return home about six o'clock. Before dinner, precisely forty minutes before dinner, he would embark on the "circuit," a one-mile walk around a nearby park. He would often be accompanied by one or both sons. After supper, he would go to his study for a few more hours of work unless it was Monday, Wednesday, or Friday. On these evenings, "The Lone Ranger" was broadcast at 7:30. Fuller and his sons would gather to listen. It was his favorite program. The evening would end with everybody on the big bed, where Claire would read a chapter or two from the current book: *Wind in the Willows*, *Alice in Wonderland*, or Laura Ingalls Wilder in the early years; the *Leatherstocking Tales*, Robert Louis Stevenson, or *Lorna Doone* as the boys grew older.

The routine was varied on weekends. Fuller came home at four o'clock on Saturday. The family would gather to pore over the movie listings, and an offering would be chosen. His taste tended to comedy and adventure. The early show would be attended, followed invariably by dinner at the Athens Olympia Restaurant, where he ordered lamb *en brochette*. Sunday was reserved for entertaining. Visiting dignitaries, fellows, and students would be invited for the midday meal. Afterward, it was outside for leaf-raking or other yard work. Sunday evening featured soup, cold cereal, and fruit, accompanied by Amos and Andy, Jack Benny, or George Burns and Gracie Allen.

Two weeks in June and the entire month of August were spent at Wilmurt Lake. Life here was unregimented and relaxed. Albright spent his time reading, supervising outside projects, and fly fishing. This seems to have been his one avocational passion. It was not prevented by his disability. He is said to have joked that his tremor gave "just the right action" to a wet fly.

Albright's personal habits were uncomplicated. He did not smoke, and he drank sparingly. He was not a heavy reader. His wife once noted that his favorite book was *War and Peace*, and that if he ever had a daughter, he would surely name her Natasha. He was devoted to the writings of Winston Churchill. His sons, however, recall lighter fare. To them, his favorite book was *A Wedding Gift* by John Taintor Foot, the story of an ill-fated "fly-fishing honeymoon."

It was a happy family. His children recall him fondly. They remember little in the way of father-son chats, disciplinary sessions, or undue pressure to follow in his footsteps. There were the usual chemistry sets and subscriptions to *Scientific American* at Christmas, but both boys indicate that it didn't take. Claire was in charge of family affairs. Fuller was free to do his work. There was mutual respect and affection throughout.

Against this background is a record of scientific achievement unequalled in the history of clinical investigation. Fuller Albright wrote 118 papers. An extraordinary number of these are significant contributions. Early studies with Joseph C. Aub and Walter Bauer described the renal effects of parathormone using the now-classic technique of the complete balance study. He described postmenopausal osteoporosis and the benefits of estrogen. He described vitamin D-resistant rickets and its treatment with large doses

Fuller Albright at Massachusetts General Hospital

of vitamin D. He described renal tubular acidosis and its treatment with alkali. He developed the treatment of hypoparathyroidism with vitamin D and dihydrotachysterol. He complemented and extended the findings of Henry Turner on gonadal dysgenesis. He described the syndrome of polyostotic fibrous dysplasia, *café-au-lait* pigmentation, and precocious puberty, and developed the concept of end organ resistance to hormone action in the example of pseudohypoparathyroidism. He described Klinefelter's syndrome, drew attention to the triad of amenorrhea, galactorrhea, and pituitary tumor, and developed the first clear understanding of the pathophysiology of congenital adrenal hyperplasia. He conceptualized the pathophysiology of Cushing's syndrome. He was the first one to suggest that a combination of estrogen and progesterone might act as a contraceptive. He described band keratopathy and the milk-alkali syndrome. He studied and clarified the metabolic antecedents of kidney stones. He developed a rational therapy for dysfunctional uterine bleeding. There is more, but the picture is clear.

These triumphs received wide recognition and honor. He was elected president of the American Society for Clinical Investigation in 1943-44, and was made president of the Endocrine Society in 1946-47. He was awarded an honorary degree from his alma mater, Harvard College, in 1955, the youngest man ever to be so recognized. These and the many other prizes and honors that came his way, however, were small recompense in the face of a growing apprehension that Parkinson's disease was eroding his intellectual power. He resolved to do something about it.

ર્અ   ર્અ   ર્અ

In 1952, Dr. Irving Cooper reported that patients with Parkinson's disease could be improved with an experimental operation called "chemopalidectomy" in which small amounts of alcohol were injected into the part of the brain that was responsible for the tremor and rigidity of the disease. Fuller became determined to undergo the procedure. By this time, he was indeed severely incapacitated. He was unable to cut his food, dress himself, open or close doors, write, or speak intelligibly. It was this last impairment that he found intolerable and wished most to be rid of. His spirit, however, remained undaunted. The force of his will can be appreciated in the following excerpt from a remembrance by his son, Read, delivered at a memorial service many years later. It explains much of what happened next.

"I will always remember his last walk to Big Rock Lake, a mile and a half from Wilmurt. It was in 1952, and the hurricanes of the previous year had left the trail obliterated and impassable with a tangle of windfalls. Nevertheless, his two sons were called forth of a summer afternoon and, in Walter Mitty fashion, it was announced: 'We're going through!' You couldn't call it walking, but he was pushed, pulled, carried, wedged, and slid the mile and a half to the isolated lake. When we arrived near dusk, he took one brief, meaningful, and I'm sure all-encompassing look at the lake, and we headed back. The sun was well down ere we sighted the landing at Wilmurt Lake that night. Pop had decided he was going to Big Rock, had set his course, and had gone. It was his last trip."

This same determination now set into motion a train of events that led to a tragic denouement. Parkinson's disease had robbed Fuller Albright of his options. It had cost him his independence and now was threatening his career.

Something had to be done, and there was only one thing that appeared to offer any solution. Still, all advice was against the operation. His physician advised against it, his consulting neurologist advised against it, and the operating surgeon advised against it. But he had decided. He had set his course, and was "going through."

The surgery was performed in June 1956. Initially, the results were favorable. He was free of tremor and rigidity on the left side, could walk better, stood more erect, and could perform useful acts with the left hand. But on the afternoon of the seventh postoperative day at three o'clock, he suffered a stroke from which he would never recover. Volitional movement remained severely impeded and he never spoke again. He lived in this state for thirteen years. Those who knew him well would visit frequently. Most believed that the intellectual fires still burned within. Discussions of old times casting to trout at Wilmurt or the description of a new theory of bone disease would sometimes elicit a response indicating recognition and understanding. But that was all. His work was ended. He died on December 8, 1969.

Fuller Albright's unpublished manuscript, *Uncharted Seas*, was included in a small bundle of papers and family correspondence that was donated by his wife, Claire, to the Countway Library in Boston in the fall of 1966. The original title page contained the names of both Albright and Ellsworth. The manuscript appears to have been written entirely by Albright however, and the reasons for including Ellsworth as an author, or the extent of his contribution to the work, are unknown.

Following the death of Dr. Albright, Richard J. Wolfe, curator of rare books and manuscripts at the Countway, was able to collect the bulk of Dr. Albright's professional correspondence and papers, which were contained in several filing cabinets at the Massachusetts General Hospital. Together with Mrs. Albright's earlier gift, this material is now preserved for future generations.

Little was done with the *Uncharted Seas* manuscript until several paragraphs were extracted from it for a brief article on creativity which appeared in the *Harvard Medical Alumni Bulletin* in the summer of 1988. Dr. Peter Ahrens brought this article to my attention, and I called Mr. Wolfe, who promptly sent me a photocopy of the entire manuscript. The first few pages convinced me that the manuscript should be published. Further study revealed that Albright had drawn from the text for parts of his famous presidential address before the American Society for Clinical Investigation in 1944 and for the lesser-known presidential address before the Endocrine Society in 1947. Other than the excerpts contained in these two speeches, however, the material was entirely new to me.

It was evident that Albright intended his book for the educated non-medical reader, in the same vein as Paul de Kruif's *Microbe Hunters* and Hans Zinsser's *Rats, Lice, and History*. In contrast to these other books, however, *Uncharted Seas* concentrates on the process whereby medical science progresses rather than on the results of that process. Albright's scientific philosophy is interleaved with the story of Captain Henry Martell, an enlightened hero who, out of his own curiosity and desire to advance discovery, gave himself to the cause of medical research. (Mrs. Albright, when giving the manuscript to Mr. Wolfe in 1966, remarked that her husband often told her that Martell's bravery so impressed him that he felt it should not go unrecorded.) It is an ideal book to illustrate the excitement and rewards of a career in medical science for young aspirants to the profession. It is also an ideal book for the literate of any background who wish to understand the counterpoint to mysticism, dogma, and quackery.

The manuscript, having never gotten beyond the rough draft stage, needed extensive editing to bring it into the style of Fuller Albright's other published works. The extent to which this has been successful or has failed is my responsibility alone. Two sheets were missing from the original typescript, pages 64-65 and 87-88 in this published version. To maintain the momentum of the text, I have reconstructed these by drawing from my own experience as a clinical investigator. (Scholars who recoil at this liberty can gain access to the original manuscript through the Department of Rare Books and Manuscripts of the Countway Library.) My words are indicated as such by footnotes; all of the other footnotes are the author's.

Why, it might be asked, did Fuller Albright not publish the book himself? My guess is that the deaths of Read Ellsworth, his closest friend, and Jacob Erdheim, his greatest hero, combined with the rapid progression of Parkinson's disease, took the joy from the work and made further contemplation of the project too painful. This, of course, is only speculation. The fact remains that the manuscript, nearly complete, was put aside—never to be picked up again.

᠀᠀   ᠀᠀   ᠀᠀

I owe thanks to a number of people who contributed to this project in an important way.

First, Mr. Richard Wolfe is responsible for the preservation of the manuscript and, equally important, understanding its significance. He has been immensely helpful in every phase of the reconstruction of the book. My wife Terri and son Marc read, word for word, each of seven iterations and helped me to see what was clear and what was not. Dr. Henry Burger read the penultimate version and made a number of insightful suggestions. Read and Birge Albright were gracious in their hospitality and shared memories of life with their father as well as family albums, letters, and their own writings on the subject. Dr. Ann Forbes provided important information about the work habits of Fuller Albright. Dr. Peter Kohler undertook the risk of publication and has contributed his professional knowledge and editorial skill from beginning to end. John Laursen of Press-22 checked and rechecked every fact and spelling, corrected a number of inaccuracies, and greatly improved the overall form of the book. Dr. Paul Ladenson was very helpful in finding material on Read Ellsworth. Dr. John Potts and Dr. Gerry Aurbach were instrumental in developing a mechanism for using funds generated by this book in the form of the Fuller Albright Fund, to be administered by the Endocrine Society. Mr. Scott Hunt and Ms. Lori Bell organized the fund within the structure of the Endocrine Society. The National Library of Medicine generously provided office space for the undertaking and made available all relevant materials in their extensive History of Medicine collection. Without these contributions, *Uncharted Seas* would still be in its box on the sixth floor of the Countway Library.

Concerning the funds that might be generated by the sale of the book, all agree that Fuller Albright would have used the money to develop and nurture young minds committed to a life of clinical science. Therefore, proceeds from the book beyond the costs of its publication will be deposited into the Fuller Albright Fund of the Endocrine Society. The purpose of this fund will be to support the cause of clinical investigation.

Uncharted Seas

1

Sex: Weighed, Bottled, and on the Market

In August 1929, at the Twelfth International Physiological Congress in Boston, a physician rose and quietly stated that he had purified "folliculin," female sex hormone, to the extent that he had crystals of the material. He showed lantern slides of these crystals. Their potency was so great that one gram could restore the sex cycle in more than nine million castrated rats.

"*Wunderson*," murmured a leading investigator in the field. The person in the next seat realized that something quite extraordinary had happened. The rows of scientists gathered from the physiological laboratories of the six continents, however, managed only a routine round of applause. Some turned to their programs to find the title of the next paper; others looked at their watches.

Sex, crystallized and weighed, and they only clapped! Is it more preposterous that Nero fiddled while Rome burned? Why didn't they do something? Was it because five days of listening to ten-minute papers in three languages in five different amphitheaters on subjects as widely separated as "The Chemical Study of Ch'an Su," "The Dried Venom of the

Chinese Toad," and "The Nature of Material Effective in Pernicious Anemia" had dulled their enthusiasm or their ability to grasp? In short, did they listen but not hear? Or were they merely skeptical? Were they exhibiting that notorious scientific reserve in accepting new facts? Or did they classify this contribution under the general category of "monkey glands" and thus accord it less importance? Were they just spoiled? Indeed, has the human race become so accustomed to the startling advances of recent years that it is now too blasé to be moved? Had Boston puritanism raised them above any interest in matters of sex? Perhaps it was Harvard indifference?

None of these altogether. It was more probably because this contribution represented the next logical advance in the evolution of a study which had been progressing in an orderly and scientific fashion for years. These physiologists had read about the sowing of the seed for this discovery. They had watched with interest the development of the tree, and many had taken part in its cultivation and growth. Thus, they were not startled now to see the mature tree ready to bear fruit.

More difficult to understand, now that a year has passed, is why those young ladies (species *Flapper Americana*) who constantly embarrass young physicians with questions about the latest advances in monkey glands fail to discuss this crystallized sex substance. In its potentialities, it has monkey glands backed off the map.* Sex, for all they know, is now crystallized and in a bottle. Not a word of

* The reader will soon observe that the writing of these pages was done over a period of years. It seemed of added interest not to try to obscure this fact.

interrogation from any of them, these same young ladies who, in the words of a visiting Britisher, "will talk about almost anything and about practically nothing else!"

The only plausible explanation is that they don't know about it. Their attention has been so focused on the much-advertised pseudoscience that real advances based on careful observation and animal experimentation have been entirely missed. The medical profession itself is partly to blame. It enjoys being aloof and obscure, enjoys using Latin words which the layman does not understand, enjoys mystifying the public with such terms as "endocrine gland" and "hormone." Small wonder that this study, of such tremendous human interest, has not been grasped by the untrained mind. The charlatan, on the other hand, can and does put his stuff across by high-pressure methods. This state of affairs seems a little unfair to the public.

It doesn't have to be this way. *Microbe Hunters*, by Dr. Paul de Kruif, has made bacteriology a living thing for many. Those who were frightened by terms like "bacteria" were not intimidated by "wee little beasties." This book will attempt to do the same for those who are afraid of the word "hormone."

We could do this with a sketch of the evolution of our understanding of the substances controlling sex. Studies of these materials have advanced to the point that several are ready for the first tests of their usefulness in the treatment of human ills. (Will the fruit be poisonous? Will whoopee be unconfined? Will. . . . But nobody knows yet. The interest, as you can imagine, is tremendous.) We will leave this story for others to tell.

Instead, we will sketch, in simple terms, the story of the discoveries which led to our present rather remarkable understanding of another gland of internal secretion. This gland is so small that few doctors have ever seen one on the dissecting table. It is so seldom out of order that its study, to some, has seemed of academic interest only. This little gland is so powerful, however, that its over- or underfunctioning can be fatal. Our story begins in distant centuries, sometimes in foreign lands. The people in this story are usually brilliant and often courageous. They are gentile and Jew, protestant and Catholic, "investigator" and "investigatee." If science had been controlled by Hitlerism, the story we are about to tell would not have happened; patients now living would be in their graves.

2

The Sowers of the Seed

Human knowledge does not grow only as a consequence of the contributions of a few great minds. Countless small bits of information make up the whole. Fact is added to fact, experience to experience. Small thoughts are joined to make larger ones, and these joined again. Mistakes are made and corrected. Differences of opinion arise and controversies ensue. Progress is made in the process of correcting errors. Negative results are no less valuable than positive ones. Pointing out which doors are the wrong ones is of great help to those who follow in the labyrinth of science. Demonstrating that two and two do not make five is of immense aid to the fellow who ultimately gets all the credit by showing that they do make four.

The domain of knowledge is constantly shifted, now this way, now that. Seldom can the direction be predicted. Occasionally a man appears who does predict, and a whole new section is mapped out. Some discoveries open gates to untrod areas and unloose throngs of eager investigators. Great trees then grow in ground prepared by many workers. All help. Those who open gates become heroes. Their work has a dramatic flavor. We can see in their achievements the play of enlightened minds upon facts established through the labor of a host of men less recognized. Occasionally, a great pathfinder sets aside all previous knowledge and strikes out anew.

Oliver Wendell Holmes spoke of minds as "one-story intellects, two-story intellects, and three-story intellects with skylights." "All fact collectors," he continued, "who have no aims beyond their facts are one-story men. Two-story men compare, reason, generalize, using the labors of the fact collectors as well as their own. Three-story men idealize, imagine, predict; their best illumination comes from above through the skylight."

This picture of the intellect painted by Holmes applies well to scientists. Often a three-story man has found illumination through the work of a one-story man. Tycho Brahe, throughout nearly a lifetime, sat in his laboratory night after night observing and recording the precise positions of the planets and stars in the sky. The figures meant little to him. Then, Johannes Kepler, a calculator *par excellence*, seized upon this amorphous mass of figures and forged from it the three great laws of planetary motion. This fortuitous conjunction of Tycho Brahe's patient accuracy and Kepler's ability to put two and two together and get four, the one-story intellect with the three, proved extraordinarily fruitful for science.

The development of scientific knowledge is a complex process. Many kinds of intellectual activity are required. First, there is seeing or observation. Observation leads to thought and more observation. This process of seeing and thinking about natural phenomena is called "natural science." Leonardo da Vinci, wandering on a mountain slope, found fossils of animals known to exist only in the sea. He reasoned that the mountain slope must have been raised from below the sea at some time in the distant past. This, together with other of his ideas, laid the foundations for the modern science of geology.

Another method of creating scientific knowledge is the experiment. Someone has an idea. Is it right, or is it wrong? Rather than argue about it, we can develop a set of conditions that will test the rightness or wrongness of the concept. This is an experiment. The better the experiment, the less equivocal the result. The results of a good experiment inevitably lead to more ideas, which lead to new experiments, and so it goes.

Nature, of course, makes many experiments for us. As a rule, she rarely arranges conditions so that we may learn the most from her experiments. They seldom occur at just the right place in our line of thought. Occasionally, however, they do. Archimedes, climbing into a bath while his mind was dwelling on the properties of floating bodies (even without the assistance of Ivory Soap) shouted, "Eureka!" as the bath flowed over; he had discovered the law of the buoyant effect of liquids upon objects immersed in them.

Within our own memory, the Royal Astronomer of England announced to the Royal Society of London that measurements on the light waves passing the sun during an eclipse had shown the exact bending predicted by Albert Einstein. His relativity theory had thus been verified. It was a momentous event in the history of science. Alfred North Whitehead said that, "A great adventure in thought had at length come safe to shore." In spite of such timely natural experiments, man has taken largely to making his own. The progress of science attests to his ingenuity.

Science, as we know it, began with Pythagoras in the sixth century B.C. He was the first to sense the value of numbers. He probably foresaw, though dimly, the role that mathematics would play in the development of science. Plato, who came after him, was also a mathematician. His influence, like that of Pythagoras, remains strong. Plato's great pupil, Aristotle, founded the science of biology, the study of living beings, in the fourth century B.C. His great mind reached out in all directions. Vast numbers of facts were stored in an encyclopedic comprehension. His was the method of observation, the method of natural science. His philosophy emphasized classification instead of measurement. Aristotle was imitated by most who followed him, and his ideas and methods were transmitted, little changed, to the Middle Ages.

During the Middle Ages, Aristotelian logic (as interpreted by the Church) produced an enormous amount of metaphysical argument about the nature of things. There was endless talk, speculation, and interpretation. There were few experiments. First accepted by the Church and later rejected, Aristotle exercised a pervading influence on thought for more than 2000 years. Under his spell, scholars classified, reclassified, and talked. They did not measure or experiment. It is said that in A.D. 1500 people knew less than Archimedes had known in 212 B.C.

The Renaissance brought a new attitude. There was a revolt against authority, against accepted views. Old dogma was cast aside. Men began to ask whether the metaphysical speculation of the Middle Ages really led to new truths or only to more metaphysics. This skepticism set the stage for the science of the sixteenth century. Men were learning to appeal to fact as determined by experiment and measurement. They were abandoning the old methods of classification and conjecture. Abelard, who lived in the Middle Ages, foreshadowed the attitude of the Renaissance when he said that, "By doubt we are led to enquire, by enquiring we perceive the truth."

One morning late in the sixteenth century Galileo, high atop the leaning tower of Pisa, dropped a ten-pound object and a one-pound object at the same time. Aristotelian doctrine declared that they would fall at different speeds. When Galileo's weights crashed simultaneously into the ground, the assembled scholars could only retire and scratch their heads. Was it possible that Aristotle could be wrong? Soon thereafter, Galileo proclaimed that a standing body will continue to stand unless a force is applied to it; that a moving body will continue to move in a straight line until some force is applied to slow it or change its direction. In one great stroke, this simple statement burst the bonds that had restrained the progress of physics for two thousand years.

At the same time Francis Bacon, Galileo's contemporary in England, was formulating new laws of science and clarifying the process of induction and the experimental method. Science jumped forward. Mathematics experienced a renaissance of its own through the work of Galileo, Descartes, Huygens, Newton, and Leibnitz. Physics and chemistry advanced as a consequence. With the growth of the sciences came the invention of new tools and instruments for doing experiments. The triumph of the experimental method was not long delayed.

Anatomy, the science of the structure of the animal body, was well advanced when the nineteenth century began. Physiology, the science of the function of the body, was far behind. Physiology is the study of the processes which take place in each organ. It tries to understand why these processes occur and what they contribute to the workings of the body as a living whole. Two factors account for the relatively slow development of physiology. First, in contrast with anatomy, in which observation is much and experiment is little, physiology is a science in which observation is important but experiment is essential. It was not until the experimental method matured that physiology could grow. Second, chemistry and physics are necessary prerequisites for physiological study. Mathematics, chemistry, and physics, the handmaidens of physiology, had to reach a certain stage of development before real progress could be made.

Physiology was in a nebulous state as late as the first half of the nineteenth century. It is not important that the reader should understand exactly which facts were known at the time and which facts, today the common knowledge of school children, were entirely unknown or only guessed at. Many processes of the body which we now comprehend fully were thought to be quite incapable of scientific explanation. They were attributed to "vital force." Laboratories were rare. The opportunity for investigation was small. There were comparatively few men engaged in scientific work. As only yesterday with psychology, there was much talk and little established fact.

Gradually, through the contributions of a few great men, the functions of the heart, vessels, nerves, muscles, and kidneys began to be understood. One of these great men was François Magendie, the most eminent French physiologist of the early nineteenth century. Although he believed that certain life processes could never be subjected to experiment, he did believe in trying. Becoming the apostle of physiological experiment, he performed hundreds of experiments with his own hands. His example had far-reaching influence. As a consequence, physiology changed. One of Magendie's pupils would carry the torch of experimental science far beyond Magendie's dreams. This pupil, by his labors and keen deductions, would open the gate to one of the greatest and most fruitful fields in all of physiology.

In 1813, when great numbers of Frenchmen were still scrambling about over Europe fighting with Napoleon from Spain to Russia, a child named Claude Bernard was born in the quiet little village of St. Julien. St. Julien lies in the heart of the ancient sun-warmed province of Beaujolais, famous of old, as it is today, for its wines. Bernard's father, like almost everyone else in the province, was a grape-grower. The family lived on a small estate. Claude proved to be a bright boy and, after preliminary instruction by the village curé and a few years at the little Jesuit college at Villefranche, he was sent to the university at Lyon. Though he progressed well there, he stopped his studies for some unknown reason and worked as a pharmacist's assistant for two years. He was very observant, and his critical faculties were stimulated by the transparent folly of many of the concoctions prepared by the druggist.

He had a flair for writing, and harbored literary and dramatic aspirations. These took shape in a musical comedy (or the nineteenth-century counterpart thereof) called *La Rose du Rhone*. It enjoyed considerable success. Thus encouraged, Bernard turned to more serious literature and wrote a historical drama called *Arthur de Bretagne*. Realizing that he must go to the French capital to achieve literary fame, he discussed his ambition with two young friends.

The three agreed to go at once to Paris. Although they started separately, Sir Michael Foster tells how they met by chance, years later, in front of the Pantheon. Bernard's two friends had not fared badly. One was a bishop, and the other a director of railways. Bernard had not fared badly either, but he was not a playwright.

Upon arriving in Paris, the young writer, armed with a letter from his professor in Lyon, went to see the greatest critic of the day, François Girardin. This gentleman, learning of Bernard's training in the pharmacy, urged the young man to confine his writing to a spare-time avocation. He suggested the profession of medicine as a more sustaining means of livelihood. He pictured clearly enough the financial difficulties sure to be encountered by a young provincial aspiring to a literary life. Since the elder Bernard had suffered a recent financial catastrophe, Claude was persuaded. He pocketed his manuscript and turned to the study of medicine.

Bernard found a garret in the Latin Quarter and, absorbed in his new studies, managed to live in contented poverty. His house was only a few doors from that where Guillotin created his famous invention and tested it on the necks of sheep. Bernard attacked his studies with keen enthusiasm. Anatomy provided elements which appealed to his penchant for exactness. Physiology fired his imagination with plans for experiments. The passion for a literary life faded and, ultimately, blinked out.

His genius, as is usually the case, was not recognized during his years as a student. He was known to have a quick perception and a full imagination, but manual dexterity was generally agreed to be his most conspicuous strength. After receiving his degree, he established a small private laboratory in the Rue Saint Jacques. He could not attract enough students, however, to make the laboratory profitable, and it failed. He continued to seek opportunity for experimental work. His mind was full of projects stimulated, in large part, by the talk he heard around him. Much of the talk seemed to be, and was, utter nonsense.

Bernard took a position as intern at the old Hotel Dieu. He soon attracted the attention of François Magendie. Magendie was impressed with his facility in preparing demonstrations. He chose him for his assistant. This was the opportunity that Bernard had been seeking. Though he was not yet free to work as he wished, a beginning was made, and substantive contributions to medical knowledge began to emerge. Experiments were performed on the physiology of nerves, salivary secretion, digestion in the stomach and intestines, the actions of pancreatic juice, the control of vascular tone, and the function of the liver. Starting always with an idea, he devised an experiment which would test it.

Holmes would have credited him with much light from above. His imagination was ever afire, except in the laboratory where, by contrast, he was all studious observation, seeing everything and understanding much that he saw. The following quotation from one of his papers is revealing: "Put off your imagination, as you take off your overcoat, when you enter the laboratory; put it on again, as you do your overcoat, when you leave the laboratory. Before the experiment and between whiles, let your imagination wrap you round; put it right away from you during the experiment itself lest it hinder your observing power."

Experiment followed experiment. The young student possessed a remarkable ability to estimate the importance of what he observed. He often turned aside from the main direction of his studies to test something which had occurred to him during an experiment. Seldom did he do so without profitable result. He was rarely led into the blind alleys that so many experimenters encounter. He possessed a true three-story intellect. Magendie once said to him, "You are a better man than I."

Claude Bernard became professor of general physiology at the Sorbonne, a member of the Academie Française, and, following Magendie's death, professor at the College de France. He was an excellent teacher. It is his experimental work, however, that captures our interest, and one series of experiments in particular.

While laboring on the thesis for his doctor's degree, Bernard discovered that cane sugar injected into the bloodstream was not used by the body. It was promptly discarded in the urine. If the cane sugar was treated with digestive juice and then injected into the bloodstream, however, it was used quite readily. A long series of experiments followed. He discovered that when the blood going into the liver contained little or no sugar, the blood coming out of the liver could contain sugar in abundance. He demonstrated that the sugar in blood was glucose, and that it could be formed in the liver from a starch-like substance which he termed "glycogen" (glucose-maker).

He made these studies known to the scientific world in 1848. He described the process by which the liver pours a substance directly into the blood for use in distant tissues. He likened this activity to the secretion of a gland. Glands, however, secreted their products into a duct. The secretions of the salivary glands, for example, issued through their ducts into the mouth. The digestive secretions of the pancreas flowed through ducts into the intestine. There was, however, no duct into which the liver secreted sugar. It seemed to be a "ductless gland." Bernard described the process as "internal secretion," or secretion into the bloodstream. This was a new concept for physiology. It opened a gate and, as we shall see, revealed new terrain that has proved to be among the most fertile and fascinating in all physiology.

Before carrying the reader into the field of the ductless glands, it will be well to make clear certain terms. Endocrinology is the study of the ductless glands. An endocrine gland is one which, without the aid of a duct, secretes a substance directly into the bloodstream. The substances produced by these glands are called internal secretions, or "hormones" (from the Greek word for messenger). They are among the most powerful substances known to man. In some instances their potency transcends credence. They govern such diverse and extraordinary phenomena as the rate of fuel utilization by the body, growth, physical activity, emotional configuration, sex, and the degree of maleness (or femaleness), among other things.

Although the author does not wish to offend the intellect of his reader by overexplaining a simple concept, it will perhaps be useful to introduce a metaphor which will be enlarged upon later to explain the workings of the body in certain specific and complex situations. Instead of a three-dimensional affair with various organs connected by a circulatory system, think of the body as a well-organized, two-dimensional industrial country that is dependent on a canal system for transportation. The ductless glands are factories located along the canals (the bloodstream). Their products (hormones) are set afloat on the canals to be delivered to various towns (organs) or to other factories (glands).

Some of the products are earmarked for only one town, while others are distributed to almost every town and seem to have an effect on nearly every household in the country. Several of the factories produce such important goods for the community that, were they to shut down, the whole land would be ruined. The products of other factories, while not necessary for survival, add much to the quality of life. Were one or another of these factories to shut down, it is not certain that a plebiscite would vote for continued existence.

Following Bernard's demonstration of the internal secretion of the liver, an English physician, Thomas Addison, showed that an extraordinary and fatal condition was produced by disease of the adrenal glands, two ductless glands located one on top of each kidney. That was in 1854. In 1856, an American physician of French descent, Charles Brown-Séquard, removed the adrenal glands from animals and produced the symptoms of Addison's disease. The animals died. These three men—Bernard, Addison, and Brown-Séquard—were the early workers in the new field of endocrinology.

Other workers soon joined in. In 1901 the great Russian physiologist, Ivan Petrovich Pavlov, found that the introduction of acid into the small intestine, just below the stomach, caused the pancreas to pour its digestive secretions into the small intestine. It was thought that this was accomplished by a reflex action through the nervous system.

In 1902, however, two of England's most eminent physiologists, William M. Bayliss and Ernest H. Starling, showed that this action occurred when all nervous connection between intestine and pancreas had been severed. How then did the pancreas know when its secretions were needed in the intestine? Could the acid be absorbed into the bloodstream and carried as a messenger to the pancreas? They injected acid into the blood. Nothing happened. Perhaps the acid caused the lining of the intestine to liberate a substance which, in turn, entered the bloodstream and was thus carried to the pancreas.

An experiment was designed to test this hypothesis. Bayliss and Starling ground up some of the lining of the small intestine and treated it with acid. This was injected into the blood, and the pancreas promptly poured its secretion into the small intestine. It was now plain that food and acid, discharged from the stomach into the small intestine, caused the small intestine to send a chemical messenger (a hormone) to the pancreas by way of the bloodstream. The pancreas responded with its secretions, which are necessary for the digestion of food. This hormone, called "secretin" by Bayliss and Starling, affects only one gland, the pancreas, and only when its secretions are needed for digestion.

This discovery was a great advance in our understanding of physiology. Claude Bernard had opened a gate and prepared the field. The early sowers had done their work. The seeds began to grow, and a flock of eager gardeners hastened there to attend them.

3

The Growth of the Parathyroid Tree

Many harvests have come and gone since the sowing of the first seeds that founded the new science of endocrinology. Have these seeds grown into useful fruit-bearing trees of knowledge, or into useless weeds?

Let us close our eyes and be wafted away to the realm of endocrinology. When we open our eyes, we see a veritable forest of trees. Closer inspection suggests an orchard, rather than a forest, in that each tree has been cultivated. Still closer inspection suggests an arboretum, in that each tree is different.

A few large, mature trees have abundant fruit that is being picked by eager consumers. Other trees, equally mature with obviously ripened fruit, have little demand for their bounty. Some trees are just sprouting; others are more advanced but still immature. Some are in full bloom but still barren; others have fruit which, although not yet ripe, is being advertised for sale prematurely. There are weeds in abundance, but it is pleasing to find that many have been uprooted and that the others are in the process of being destroyed.

One grove of trees is behind a high stone wall. It bears a large sign saying, "No Admittance, per Order of the Watch and Ward Society." These are the trees which have to do with sex. A glimpse through the gate shows that they are flourishing and bearing fruit. Will the fruit be forbidden? But that is another story.

At the foot of each tree are gathered groups of men, apparently the nurserymen of the individual trees. The groups vary greatly in size, but each tree has obviously benefited from the labor of many. Here and there a nurseryman rushes from tree to tree, applying his skill to each in turn. What he has learned in the cultivation of one tree, he applies to another. Many different languages are spoken by these horticulturists, but English is heard frequently amid the medley of German, French, Russian, and Chinese.

What is this tree apart by itself? Its label reads, "Parathyroid Glands." It seems to be as mature as any tree in the grove and has the appearance of having had a very rapid growth. The fruit looks ripe, but nobody seems to want it. But wait, here comes a poor fellow *in extremis* and, wondrous to behold, he is much improved after eating the fruit. The little group of gardeners look on and seem intensely pleased. They are delighted with the tree in its own right, but the occasional saving of one of these lost sheep by the fruit of the tree increases their otherwise purely academic satisfaction. What difference does it make that other nearby trees attract more attention and save thousands (for example, yonder large tree marked "Pancreatic Islands," the fruit of which is tied up in little packages labeled "Insulin")? Let us approach this isolated group who, with perseverance, tend their tree whose fruit, so little in demand, is so precious to those in need of its healing powers.

"*Was ist die Ursache dafür?*" (What is the cause of this?) These words meet our ears as we approach. They are spoken by the head gardener for this tree, the fruit of which can save lives. The appearance of the head gardener is so arresting that, for the moment, we turn our full attention to him. He has a huge frame. Although he is not excessively tall, his hips are as high as an average man's chest. The hands are large and deft. His eyes smile from behind gold-rimmed spectacles as he expostulates in a somewhat high-pitched voice, "*Manche Leute sehen sehr gut aber sie schauen nicht an.*" (Many people see well but neglect to look.)

You engage him in conversation. You try English first. He does not seem to understand. You try German. Your grammar is poor, but he understands perfectly. You begin to consider yourself quite a linguist. Later you learn that so many American students have come to his laboratory that he has become an expert on German as spoken by Americans. As you get to know him better, you find that he understands English quite well but enjoys deciphering broken German. To your surprise, you understand his German without difficulty; it is clear and simple. You are amazed to discover that German is his second language. He is, in fact, a Jew who was born in a small Polish town. You picture a countrified boy arriving in Vienna, the most sophisticated of all European capitals, and you wonder what qualities transformed him into the greatest of living pathologists, Professor Jacob Erdheim.

If you go to his laboratory as a student and stay for one year, you will discover several surprising things about the man. He is shy. It may be many months before you break through his reserve. He lives alone in a single room in the

City Hospital of Vienna. He eats simple hospital food. He works eighteen hours a day. He regards smoking and drinking as vices. The picture is that of a rather prosaic grind. But when we analyze the characteristics which contributed to the growth of the tree, other qualities emerge.

An uncanny ingenuity is found to be coupled with his industry, a rare combination of perseverance and genius in one man. Outside recreations are not lacking. He is fond of music; everyone in Vienna is, or at least claims to be. One day at the autopsy table, perhaps after some routine piece of work such as describing the findings in a pair of lungs riddled with tuberculosis, he surprises you with a scholarly digression on Renaissance art. You learn that each year the professor spends his month's vacation in Italy. Then, suddenly, thoughts of Michelangelo and the beauty of the Sistine Chapel are interrupted as a brain abscess or some other finding of interest dispels pleasant fantasy with grim fact.

Then there are digressions on what, to the professor, seems to be the most amazing of all species: the itinerant American medical student. Himself shy and thorough, the Professor regards these young men as forward and, often, superficial. Hundreds of them flock to Vienna every year.* Some represent the best that America has to offer; others are merely charlatans seeking a degree from one of the oldest universities on the continent so that it can be displayed in their offices.† This degree may be obtained by any physician who pays for a few months of graduate courses. He need not attend the courses and there are no examinations.

* Needless to say, this part was written in the pre-*Putsch* days.

† The University of Vienna was founded in 1064 by Rudolph IV; the University of Prague was founded in 1347.

Those who really wish to learn come to the pathological demonstrations of the professor. Erdheim is interested in Americans. He has never been to their land, but he reads everything about it that he can find. He probably has collected more misinformation on the subject than any living being outside of Russia.

You have come to work with this extraordinary man, armed, in all likelihood, with several letters of introduction from bigwigs at home. Do not be surprised that the wheels are not immediately set rolling. The answer to this paradox, if you are observant, will soon appear. On the continent, there is a considerable traveling population of American doctors who, in a six-week trip, expect to visit the eight or ten investigators whose names mean most at home. The challenge is increased by the need to work this in between the night life of Paris and the beer halls of Munich. This is quite pleasant for the visitors, but a great waste of time for the visitees. Different laboratories have developed different antidotes for this menace. Professor Erdheim has a protective armor of cold politeness. "Yes, of course you can work here. Anybody is free to come and work." The conversation ends. Demonstrate that you mean business by several months of hard work, however, and the atmosphere warms by a few degrees.

Then one day, out of a clear sky, the Professor asks you to come into his private study and talk with him about your work. You enter. You have never seen so many specimens. Jars of every size and description line the walls. All are carefully labeled. You are surprised to find a little nest of mice in one corner. They seem quite tame. The Professor does not notice them. If his attention is directed their way, he may give some personal observation on the habits of mice. Six hours pass before you finally emerge from his room. You are hungry and realize that a meal has been entirely forgotten. You have seen many unusual microscopic slides and you have learned many things which have never been recorded on paper. You feel inspired. You resolve that in the future, "*Was ist die Ursache?*" will be a question ever in your mind.

Spring comes. A lilac sprig may give rise to a digression on Luther Burbank, the American naturalist, and his methods. One cold morning you arrive at the laboratory and find all the windows open. You shiver and rush around to close them. The Professor arrives, and it becomes apparent that closing the windows was a mistake. You wish you could vanish into thin air. You learn that it is time for the swallows to arrive. In a few days they are there, flying in and out of the windows, nesting in the corners. In a few weeks the young are hatched, some of which are transported to new artificial nests, to which they will return the following year. The Professor has one put in a cubbyhole in his desk. You are amazed to see a big able-bodied diener rushing around catching flies. Toward evening he brings his catch to the Professor. The Professor takes the flies and, with a pin, feeds them one by one to the young swallows. This is all very well, you expostulate with the Professor, but time is money. He is highly amused. "*In Wien hat man viel Zeit aber kein Geld.*" (In Vienna, one has plenty of time but no money.) Several years later, during the American Depression, this aphorism will often come to mind.

Perhaps you wonder what this extraordinary man, living such a simple existence, does with the money he earns from his demonstrations to American students. Rumor has it that he is an ardent Zionist and gives all his pennies to that cause. It rings true.

25

What, then, are the personal qualities of the head gardener? A natural industriousness which has been increased by his hermitic existence and great physical power. A capacity for observation which uncovers new facts where others see nothing of note. A curiosity which asks, *"Was ist die Ursache?"* ten times a day. An extraordinary reasoning power which finds answers for this question more often than not.

But what about the tree? Which of these horticulturists planted it and started it on its way?

Our story begins with anatomy, the study of the structure of the body. The science of anatomy naturally preceded that of physiology, just as the heavenly bodies were mapped and named before the relation of one to the other was understood. You will not be surprised to learn that the science of anatomy has been nearly at a standstill for many years. Careful dissections of all parts have been made; microscopic sections of all structures have been prepared; the characteristics of each cell have been described. What is left for the anatomist to do? What does a professor of anatomy do when he is not lecturing? Either he does nothing, in which case he does not deserve his chair, or he busies himself trying to understand the function of some of these cells; he metamorphoses into a physiologist. Several of the best gardeners in our enchanted forest occupy chairs of anatomy.

The first step in the development of our knowledge about a gland is the anatomic description of the gland itself. Ivar Sandström, a Swedish anatomist, first identified the parathyroid glands in 1880. They are in the neck, four of them, in direct contact with the thyroid gland. Why weren't they discovered sooner? It is probably because the largest diameter of a normal parathyroid gland is about one-half centimeter. Add to this the fact that the neck contains many nodular structures of this size which can be distinguished from the parathyroid glands only by microscopic examination. When it is realized that most doctors, even today, have never seen one, our respect for Sandström increases. The following quotation from his paper, "On a New Gland in Man and Several Mammals," is of interest:

"The existence of a hitherto unknown gland in animals that have so often been a subject of anatomical examination called for a thorough approach to the region around the thyroid gland even in man, although the probability of finding something hitherto unrecognized seemed so small that it was exclusively with the purpose of completing the investigations rather than with the hope of finding something new that I began a careful examination of this region. So much the greater was my astonishment therefore when in the first individual examined I found on both sides at the inferior border of the thyroid gland an organ of the size of a small pea, which, judging from its exterior, did not appear to be a lymph gland, nor an accessory thyroid gland, and upon histological examination showed a rather peculiar structure."

A second observation made by Sandström is less profound, is not directly related to the parathyroid tree, and undoubtedly has been made many times before and since. This observation found expression in a letter from Sandström to his sister dated August 8, 1880: ". . . I accepted an invitation from Stockholm to attend the meeting of the natural scientists [naturforskarmotet] in order that I might do my part so that we Swedes should not succumb to our guests—which later on proved not to be the case at all. . . . One should, of course, at a personal meeting of so many

27

men who devote themselves to science, be inclined to expect less of a hurried reading of more or less unimportant 'products of genius' whose creators in any case would not forget to publish them, if they are of any value, than rather a friendly exchange of thoughts and a trustful communication of personal experiences and impressions. Nothing of the kind was seen. . . . Everyone seemed to be there with the intention of showing what 'discoveries' he had made, and at the same time giving the astonished world the opportunity to have a look at the fortunate discoverer. But for the discovery itself, for the revealed truth, the interest was little or none."*

We know little more of this keen observer of anatomy, a man who made his important discovery at the age of twenty-five while still a medical student: a man who returned to his maker at thirty-five years of age, one job, at least, well done.

Sandström's letter to his sister was prophetic. The world was not startled. In fact, it paid no attention to his discovery. The seed was sown but lay dormant. Then, eleven years later, a series of coincidences started the parathyroid tree on a course of rapid growth.

It was well that Sandström called his new glands "*glandulae parathyroideae*," emphasizing by the prefix *para* (along side of) their location near the thyroid gland. Were it not for this proximity, our knowledge about them would not have advanced so fast.

One of the best ways to demonstrate the activity of an endocrine gland is to destroy it and study the consequences. In retrospect, it is clear that the consequences of

* Translated by Dr. Carl M. Siepel.

destroying the parathyroid glands were observed many times before 1880, before the existence of these glands was even known. Here is where the "para-" comes in. The story starts like this.

People live in all sorts of places; among them are places devoid of iodine. This circumstance is regularly associated with an enlargement of the thyroid gland called a goiter. When a goiter is very large, it attracts the attention of a surgeon who eagerly, and for the most part satisfactorily, deals with it. "For the most part" is the important phrase. Occasionally, after such an operation, a patient would develop a condition known as tetany. Never mind what sort of an ailment tetany is; that will come in due course. The natural assumption was that tetany was caused by the removal of the thyroid gland. This belief was strengthened when it was found that tetany developed less often if part of the thyroid gland was left in place.

Why did tetany follow the removal of the thyroid gland in some cases and not in others, and in some animals and not in others? The reader undoubtedly has guessed the answer. One of the gardeners that we saw by the tree was a Frenchman by the name of Émile Gley. He showed, in 1891, that tetany develops only when the tiny parathyroid glands are destroyed during the operation. Animals whose parathyroid glands are situated at a safe distance from the thyroid gland do not develop tetany when the thyroid gland is removed. Thus, if part of the thyroid gland is left in place when the goiter is removed, one or more of the parathyroid glands may be left behind and tetany thereby prevented.

The medical profession had been barking up the wrong tree. To revert to the simile of our industrial land, it isn't the product of the thyroid factory that prevents tetany, but the product of its four little annexes, the parathyroid factories.

The final proof of this was established in 1906. It had been shown by Gley that removal of the parathyroid glands caused tetany in animals, but this had not yet been demonstrated in man. Presumably it would be true, but in science, presumption must be checked. The drama unfolds in Vienna. There are three actors: Erdheim, a diener, and a patient with goiter. The patient enters the Allgemeines Krankenhaus and is operated upon. He dies with, and of, tetany. Professor Erdheim does the post-mortem examination. No parathyroid factories can be found. But that does not mean they are not there.

To answer that question, Erdheim and his diener remove all of the tissue from the patient's neck and divide it into small pieces. Each piece is then cut into hundreds of thin microscopic slices. They do nothing for several months but make slices. At last, all of the slices are prepared. Each slice must now be examined under the microscope for evidence of parathyroid tissue. The professor goes to the Tyrol. For several months he looks at slices. At last he is satisfied that, in this patient, no parathyroid tissue was present. He concludes that all of the parathyroid tissue must have been removed with the goiter. His glasses have to be changed several diopters because of eyestrain. The case is reported in connection with some other work. At the end of the report comes the simple statement: "Sections were made of the entire neck region, and no parathyroid tissue was found." Six months hard work, two diopters change in glasses, a simple statement. Science advances a little.

But what is tetany? Alas! It will be convenient again to resort to metaphor. Before bewildering the reader further by metaphors within metaphors (mixed and otherwise), we had better liquidate the enchanted forest and, in so doing, step into a new chapter.

So far, little ground has been covered. What has been described, the discovery of the parathyroid glands and the fact that their absence leads to a condition known as tetany, is the kind of knowledge that inevitably follows the general progress of science. In the next chapter, we examine an advance that was far ahead of its appointed time, an advance which depended upon the brilliance of one observer with a three-story intellect and a good skylight.

4

Wherein the Connection is Made Between a Gland and an Element

What, then, is tetany? The "why" of tetany we have already discussed. Now for the "how." How does it happen? In the first place, it has nothing to do with tetanus, or lockjaw, a condition caused by an infection with a specific type of bacteria. Our kind of tetany follows the removal of the parathyroid glands.

Think of the body in terms of a telegraph company. The brain and spinal cord represent a large central exchange which takes in and sends out messages. The nerves are the wires which transmit the messages. Many of the messages are destined for muscles. These messages usually say the same thing: "Please contract." All of these messages are normally sent from, or through, the central exchange.

There are, however, ways of sending messages without going through the central exchange. For example, the mere pinch of a nerve can start a message along which ultimately stimulates the contraction of a muscle at the other end. An electrical stimulus to a nerve trunk will cause a similar response. Some nerves are so accustomed to carrying one message that they do so under all circumstances. For instance, the nerve to the eye carries messages that are only interpreted in terms of light. A patient who is having an eye removed may see a flash of light at the moment the optic nerve is cut. In the same way, nerves that usually carry messages instructing muscles to contract will do so whether or not the message originated in the central exchange.

Tetany is what happens when most of the messages to muscles originate outside of the central exchange. A patient with this malady requires less electricity than a normal person to start a message down a nerve. Some of the nerves may even transmit a message in response to a mechanical "tap." This would not occur under normal circumstances. The whole telegraph system, in other words, is on the alert. Messages are sent out at the slightest provocation. Some wires are so busy that the muscles at the other end never get a chance to relax.

Picture an individual with a scar in the neck where the thyroid gland has been removed and the parathyroid glands destroyed in the bargain. Arms and legs are in a state of spasm. The patient is wheezing, because the muscles of the voice box are so tight that air passes with difficulty. Death is imminent. To this person, any useful knowledge about the parathyroid glands is of interest. No questions would be asked from whence the knowledge came, be it from gentile or Jew.

But why this increased excitability of nerves? The answer to this question is still many pages on. First we must clear up a much more fundamental point by journeying back to Vienna: to Erdheim, rats, and rats' teeth. This clarification depended upon four unlikely "ifs" coming together at one time and place. Consider these "ifs:" if the parathyroid glands of rats were not situated as they are (unlike the case in almost all other animals, they can be removed without affecting the thyroid gland); if rats were not less susceptible than most animals to tetany (they can live a fairly normal existence without their parathyroid glands); if rats' teeth (like those of all rodents) did not continue to grow like the rings of a tree throughout life; if Erdheim had been one of the many people who *sehen sehr gut, aber schauen nicht an.* If any of these "ifs" had been true, the parathyroid tree in the enchanted forest would still be a seedling. Fortunately, none was true. No one would have bet that "parathyroidology" could take these four jumps at once, but it did.

In the days when it was still argued whether thyroid or parathyroid deficiency caused tetany, Erdheim said to himself that, to resolve the question, an experimental animal was needed in which one type of gland could be removed without the other. It turned out that the parathyroid glands in the rat are only two in number, are just visible to the unaided eye, are situated on the surface of the thyroid gland, and can be destroyed easily by the touch of a red-hot needle. Animals treated in this way develop mild tetany. The professor sat up nights recording the number of seizures the animals had in twenty-four hours. When the animals were put away in cages, they didn't die. They continued to eat. At the end of several weeks the Professor examined them. Their teeth were a little off color. Rats' teeth normally have a translucent appearance. The teeth of these animals were opaque. *Was ist die Ursache?*

This was a difficult question to answer. Very little was known about teeth; less about rats' teeth. A technique had to be developed for cutting teeth into fine microscopic slices. Many difficulties had to be overcome. When they were, the mist cleared. The facts were simple and irrefutable. Rats' teeth, like those of the beaver, are constantly growing up from the pulp cavity and wearing off at the gnawing end. If an upper tooth, for instance, does not meet one from the opposite jaw so that it can be worn down, it will grow unchecked and ultimately pierce the neck of the animal and kill it (at least so the yarn goes).

Between the pulp cavity, where new tooth material is being laid down, and the surface which is wearing off, there is a stretch that represents a growth of several weeks. One is reminded of the cross sections of giant redwood trees that can be seen in the Natural History Museum in New York. Each ring represents the growth for one year. Dry seasons and wet seasons are expressed in thin and thick rings, respectively. The seasons can be charted accurately back to times before the birth of Christ. The same kind of record could be read in the rings of a rat's tooth. Erdheim found that from the minute the parathyroid glands were removed, the new layers of tooth contained insufficient calcium.

Further experiments were performed. The parathyroid glands were removed, a period of days was allowed to elapse, and parathyroid glands from other animals were implanted. The idea was that the hormones contained in these glands would be utilized by the recipient animals to build normal bones and teeth. Another period of days was allowed to elapse. The animals were killed. The teeth were sectioned. Reading from the "wearing off" surface inward, there was normal tooth formed before the parathyroid glands were destroyed, then tooth without calcium which was formed after the parathyroid glands were destroyed, followed by a band of normal tooth that was formed after the parathyroid gland transplant. Now that the product of the parathyroid glands can be bought in a bottle, this simple experiment has been repeated, using injections of the hormone instead of transplanted parathyroid glands.

This early experiment of Erdheim led to the concept that calcium is not deposited into growing teeth in the absence of the hormones of the parathyroid glands. This was the clue which directed the attention of all subsequent parathyroid investigators to calcium. The clue was followed in two entirely different ways by the American and Viennese schools. Both routes led to the same important discovery in the same year, 1926.

This discovery, as we shall see, deals with what occurs when there is overproduction in the parathyroid factories. We have seen that tetany results when there is underproduction, although the wherefore of tetany is yet to come.

5

Overproduction by Parathyroid Factories: Contributions of the Viennese School

That the Viennese and American schools should have proceeded along different routes is not mere chance. Vienna has been, for many years, one of the foremost centers for the study of pathology. When a person dies in a hospital in Vienna, an autopsy is performed without fuss or question. The physician in charge sees the autopsy and sees his mistakes. Gradually, mistakes become fewer.

The situation in America is different. A physician has been puzzling over a case for weeks; he has built up some sort of working hypothesis concerning the diagnosis; the patient dies because of, or in spite of, the treatment. The family gathers around. Everybody is hysterical. Nobody thinks clearly. The physician, if young and enthusiastic, attempts to get somebody to sign the necessary permission for an autopsy. The grandmother immediately suggests that the patient has already suffered enough. The physician pleads that such an examination may teach him things which will save another patient with the same condition. Perhaps a new scientific truth will be revealed that can save thousands. He may or may not be about to carry his point. The undertaker arrives. This gentleman is against the autopsy. The physician is about to lose.

Before giving in, he lowers the argument from the ethical plane on which it has until now been held, and begins to draw from an old bag of tricks. Anything is now fair. It is pointed out that all that is wanted is permission to make a small incision, only a little longer than would be needed to remove an appendix (oh yea!), or that the incision will be confined to the abdomen and that the chest and head will not be touched.* Or he may descend to even lower depths. Some interns become very expert in getting autopsies. They are seldom questioned as to their methods in this part of their job. The academic rating of hospitals depends in large measure on the percentage of autopsies they obtain.

The sympathies of the reader are probably with the patient's family; so are the sympathies of the writer. The solution is easy. Autopsies should be a matter of course, no questions asked. The physician who has missed getting an autopsy consoles himself by rationalizing and concluding that his diagnosis was right. After a few such experiences, he may give up any attempt to get autopsies, and continue to conclude that he is right. And so it is not surprising that certain conditions were known and argued in Vienna for years before their existence was even heard of by the average physician in this country.

Erdheim had shown that the products of the parathyroid factories have to do with calcium. Calcium is one of the chief components of the skeleton and of the teeth. He at once asked to be allowed to perform the autopsies on all

---

* It is hard work to get the tonsils out through an abdominal incision but it has been done.

patients who died with diseases of the bones. There is one condition of the bones which is characterized by a decrease of calcium. The bones are so soft that they can be cut with a knife. They become very much bent as a result of the force of gravity. This condition is called "osteomalacia," from the Greek words for bone (*osteon*) and softness (*malakia*).

Erdheim's efforts were immediately rewarded. Of the first eight patients with osteomalacia on whom he performed an autopsy, six had marked enlargement of all of their parathyroid factories. This was something more than pure coincidence. Was the overproduction in these factories the cause of this mysterious bone condition, or was the mysterious bone condition the cause of the overproduction?

The Professor argued, and rightly so, that since all four factories were enlarged, the enlargement must be secondary to something else, most likely to the bone condition. Sometimes one of the endocrine factories suddenly, and for no apparent reason, begins to expand and flood the market. The cause for the sudden expansion is no more understood than the cause for cancer. Such expansions are, of course, tumors. But it would be unlikely for all four parathyroid factories suddenly and simultaneously to start overproduction if there were not some demand for their product from without. Therefore, Erdheim warned, this enlargement was secondary and probably compensatory. He predicted that removal of the enlarged factories would only make matters worse. The Viennese school listened. They knew the Professor was *never*—well, scarcely ever—wrong. They followed his dictum and were correct in doing so.

But we must go back a little. The founder of cellular pathology (that is, the study of diseased tissues under the microscope) was Rudolf Virchow of Berlin. It is customary in German academic circles to make an occasion of the birthdays of their famous men. Former pupils bring out what they consider their best work in elaborate special editions or *Festschrifts*. Thus, in 1891, a *Festschrift* for Virchow's seventieth birthday was assembled and in this there appeared by a former pupil, Professor Friedrich Daniel von Recklinghausen of Strassburg, a very complete description of the skeletal changes in patients who had died of certain bone diseases.

Three of these patients died of a condition which has since been known as von Recklinghausen's disease. As in osteomalacia, the skeleton is very soft and bent because of lack of calcium compounds. There are other peculiarities, however, especially the formation of cysts in the bones. These are cavities filled with fluid. Fractures are apt to occur through these cysts. The condition, while recognized as different from osteomalacia, was often confused with it and placed in much the same category by most people. Upon this confusion hangs a story which we will come to in due time.

Who were these three patients who died of this strange condition? What manner of men were they? A butcher, a baker, a candlestick maker? Let's keep some of our interest for the individual with the disease and not dissipate it all on the disease itself.

Von Recklinghausen has given us considerable information about one of these unfortunates. Herr Bleich was a mason and a married man. In April 1888, in his fortieth year, he fell from a three-meter ladder onto his left side, and eight days later was admitted to the surgical clinic because of pain in the hip. His past history revealed that he had undergone a mercury cure for syphilis years before. It was probably not relevant to the problem at hand. When admitted to the hospital, it was uncertain whether or not he had fractured his thigh bone near the hip. These were still, of course, the horse and buggy days, before x-rays. Rest in the hospital helped. By August, he was improved enough to walk with a stick. In October, Herr Bleich slipped in the waiting room of the surgical clinic and fell against a bench, fracturing his collarbone. He was admitted to the clinic. Another fracture occurred, this time of his right upper leg, when he was given a bedpan clumsily! Examination the following summer found him emaciated and complaining of excruciating pains in many bones. There was extensive bending of the upper arms, upper legs, and one lower leg. Herr Bleich continued to fail, and died on October 4, 1889.

When Erdheim showed, in 1907, that the parathyroid factories were enlarged in osteomalacia, every pathologist in Vienna began to examine the parathyroid glands in patients with abnormalities in their bones. Isolated cases of von Recklinghausen's disease, in which only one of the parathyroid factories was enlarged, soon were found. Thus began a great controversy which was not settled until 1926. Were the single enlarged parathyroid factories in von Recklinghausen's disease the cause or the result of the bone disease?

A few bold voices from time to time pointed out that the fact that only one factory was involved meant the condition must have arisen in the affected factory. The prevailing opinion was so greatly influenced by the teachings of Erdheim in the context of osteomalacia, however, that nobody clearly recognized that what was true of osteomalacia might not be true for this similar but distinct disease.

The discussions usually ended where they started. The patients became more and more skeletonless, more and more plant-like, until finally they were mere jellyfish incapable of locomotion, in some cases dying of suffocation, unable to move the chest in respiration. Despite frequent quotation to the contrary, it should be noted that Erdheim never expressed his opinion as to whether the parathyroid enlargement is primary or secondary in von Recklinghausen's disease.

But you cannot fool all of the people all of the time. The story continues in the Viennese clinic of Professor Anton von Eiselsberg at the old Allgemeines Krankenhaus. Somewhere in this hospital must hang a portrait of Christian Billroth, one of the great figures in surgery, the first surgeon to operate in the abdominal cavity. Professor von Eiselsberg was the academic son of Billroth, and he proved worthy of the relationship. This story, however, deals with one of von Eiselberg's pupils, R. Mandl, an academic grandson of Billroth.

The year is 1924. A patient, destined to become famous, enters the clinic. His name is Albert. He is a streetcar conductor, thirty-eight years of age. He had chicken pox when he was five and measles at six. Not surprising. He contracted syphilis at nineteen. A little surprising. He fought for Emperor Franz Joseph in the Great War. He was sent home from the front when he developed pulmonary tuberculosis. This disease is so prevalent among Viennese that it is called the "*Wiener Krankheit.*" Such was Albert's background.

He began to complain of tiredness and pains in his legs and hips in 1921. These pains were made worse by movement and by sneezing and coughing. He had to give up his work and was pensioned. Various treatments were prescribed: mercury for syphilis, cod liver oil for his bones, electrical treatments for God knows what. He was also given mud baths at Schallback in the belief that the trouble was rheumatism or arthritis. The condition had its ups and downs but, like the stock market of today,* mostly its downs. X-ray studies were made in 1923. The bones were very transparent and contained cysts. Transparency means too little calcium. The cysts led to the diagnosis of von Recklinghausen's disease.

In October 1924, Albert came to the hospital on crutches. His gait was very uncertain, and his back was bent and misshapen due to weakness in the bones of the spine. The old controversy rose again: which was the cart and which was the horse? If the enlargement in the parathyroid factory is compensatory to the bone disease, treatment with extract of an animal's parathyroid glands should help. This was tried. It did not help. In December 1924, the inevitable happened. Albert stumbled and broke his leg. By this time he could not walk, stand, or sit. His urine contained a white sediment.

Perhaps the animal parathyroid extracts were not potent. Another experiment was tried. A dying man was brought to the hospital following an accident in the street. He died. As soon as the heart had stopped, Dr. Mandl removed the four parathyroid factories and transplanted them into Albert. There was no improvement.

Albert's situation was desperate. He was fast reaching the jellyfish stage. July 30, 1925 came. Dr. Mandl took the bull by the horns and operated on Albert. He found one tremendously expanded parathyroid factory and removed it. The unbelievable happened. Within the next six days the

* 1931.

white sediment, which was calcium, disappeared from the urine. The skeleton was no longer being dissolved and excreted in the urine. Soon the bone pain began to improve. By October, Albert was on crutches again. X-rays showed the bones beginning to fill up with calcium. The patient with a heretofore fatal disease had been cured. The riddle was solved. The story which began with rat's teeth ended with the saving of Albert's life. His name had been added, along with that of Herr Bleich, to the rolls of the immortal "investigatees."

The answer was unequivocal. Von Recklinghausen's disease was caused by overproduction from one of the parathyroid factories. It could be cured by removing the factory. This answer was arrived at by starting with the finished disease and gradually pulling it to pieces.

The same answer was in the process of being discovered on the other side of the Atlantic by men who didn't have such opportunities to see autopsies: men to whom von Recklinghausen's disease was all but unknown. They were even less aware of the fact that enlarged parathyroid glands were associated with it. But these men, handicapped in one way, were better favored in another. They were provided both with well-equipped laboratories and with adequate money for animal experiments and chemical determinations. Their story is very different.

6

Overproduction by Parathyroid Factories: Contributions of the American School

The ocean is not made of distilled water. It contains, besides sodium and chlorine which together make salt, certain other elements. Among these is calcium. Life started in the sea. It first consisted of a simple single-celled animal. This animal, after centuries of life in the ocean, became very particular about its external environment. It prospered only when it was surrounded by water containing the appropriate amounts of sodium, calcium, and the other elements dissolved in the sea. More complicated animals with many cells developed. Animals finally evolved with an outside coating that permitted life outside of water. Life colonized the land, but the cells in these more complex animals still needed the old external environment of the sea. This was accomplished by having the body fluids, including the blood, be of the same composition as the sea. Ages have passed. The sea has become saltier because of continued evaporation. The blood, however, retains the composition of the sea as it was when life emerged from it.

What happens if the environment of the cells is changed by changing the composition of body fluid? This fundamental question was asked by an investigator of fundamental things, Jacques Loeb. He is the same Loeb who, as head of the Department of Experimental Biology of the Rockefeller Institute, startled the already sufficiently excited world of 1916 with the artificial fertilization of frogs' eggs. Fatherless frogs: virgin birth in the laboratory! Science will catch up to religion yet. But the experiments which concern us are less sacrilegious. A muscle was taken from a living frog and surrounded with an environment of water and table salt. The muscle contracted rhythmically. Calcium was added to the environment. The muscle stopped contracting. Loeb concluded that we owe it to the calcium in our blood that our muscles are not continuously twitching.

The scene changes to Baltimore, where a great renaissance in American medicine was being enacted under the leadership of William Osler, William Welch, and William Halsted. Of these three, Welch was the pathologist. He was an academic grandson of Virchow, and a first cousin once removed, therefore, of von Recklinghausen. The present professor of pathology at Johns Hopkins University, Professor William G. MacCallum, was working with Welch in 1909. He and his associate, Carl Voegtlin, put two and two together and got four. Their reasoning went like this: the parathyroids have something to do with calcium (Erdheim and rats' teeth); calcium prevents muscles from constantly twitching (Loeb and frogs' muscles); tetany (due to too little parathyroid tissue) is associated with an increased excitability of the muscles; *ergo*, tetany is caused by too little calcium in the blood.

They put this hypothesis to the test. Dogs lost their parathyroid glands; they developed tetany. As predicted, their blood contained too little calcium. Dogs with tetany were cured when calcium was injected into the blood. Science advanced again. There was now a rational means of treating tetany in man. The patient with tetany who receives an injection of calcium and derives instant though temporary relief is indebted to the experiments of Loeb on frogs' muscles, the experiments of Erdheim on rats' teeth, and the experiments of MacCallum and Voegtlin on dogs' parathyroid glands.*

The Johns Hopkins investigators had done more than point out the cause of the increased excitability of the nerves in tetany. They furnished an accurate measuring stick. Something to measure is, as we have seen, essential for the advancement of science. The daily production of the parathyroid factories could now be monitored by measuring blood calcium; a decrease in production would be reflected in a lower blood calcium level.

Once the measuring stick for the function of a gland is in hand, the chemist's time has come. There were, of course, delays. Accurate methods for determining calcium in body fluids had to be developed. They were ready soon. Animal parathyroid factories obtained from slaughterhouses were subjected to chemical procedures designed to isolate the active principle, the hormone. The time was ripe; insulin had just been isolated. Various brews were made. Each was injected into "parathyroidless" animals and the effect on blood calcium noted. There was no working in the dark. Either the active principle was there or it was not. In 1924 it was there, and the man who made the extract was Dr. James Bertram Collip of the University of

---

* N.B. all ye who are of antivivisectionist persuasion!

Alberta, Canada. Collip was one of the nurserymen in our forest whom we saw rushing from tree to tree. Fresh from the insulin tree, he hastened to the parathyroid tree, and then was off to the sex gland trees. What he learned from one tree he applied to the next. He produced, in a neatly labeled bottle, the mysterious product of the parathyroid factories that keeps the calcium in the blood at the exact level present in sea water when life emerged from it. Our patient with tetany, thanks to Collip, could now receive injections of parathyroid extract from the factories of animals.

But Collip went on. The inquiring mind always goes on. The next step can best be understood if we recall to mind, enlarge upon, and make more fantastic our industrial country composed of communities, a canal system, telegraph services, factories, etc. We have seen that the smooth running of such a country is dependent upon four parathyroid factories situated near some of the canals, and that when these factories are working at normal activity (presumably an eight-hour day, five days a week), there is a certain and definite amount of calcium being transported back and forth in the waterways. An efficient secretary of commerce for this country could get an accurate estimate of the activity of the parathyroid factories by analyzing the amount of calcium on the inland waterways. Any interference with the output of these factories decreases the transportation of calcium and, in this very strange land, is associated with a disturbance in the telegraphic system of the whole country.

Just as most of the calcium in the body is kept in the bones, in our imaginary country it is stored in large depots; just as some calcium is in a constant process of being lost from the body by excretion in the urine, in our country some of the calcium in the waterways finds its way to the sea. The canals, however, are not directly connected with the sea. There are filtration plants (the kidneys) which allow some canal traffic to pass while other traffic is detained. Calcium passes without trouble. The amount which reaches the sea depends upon the amount being transported on the waterways. Unless imports equal losses, scarcity will result.

Therefore, if the depots of calcium are not to be depleted, the country must import calcium through its one port of entry (the gastrointestinal tract) in amounts at least equal to those lost through the filtration plants. Calcium comes into the country in food products. A shipload of milk, for example, brings in a generous supply.

Just how the products of the parathyroid factories affect the commerce of the country to promote an increased amount of calcium in circulation, is a secret which has not yet been divulged by the dictator of our land. One might guess that when the products of the parathyroid factories arrive at the calcium depots via the canals, they stimulate the workers there, in some mysterious way, to put calcium afloat. But this is conjecture. What is not conjecture is that if the parathyroid factories are destroyed by some means, such as a thunderbolt from Zeus, parathyroid products imported from other lands can act equally well to maintain the calcium on the waterways. So far, so good.

It occurred to Collip to see what would happen to our fair land if it were suddenly flooded with parathyroid products from foreign markets. Once these products were in a bottle and marketed, the experiment could be tried. The results from such experiments (on dogs) were clear. A sample of fluid taken from the inland waterways showed that the level of circulating calcium was far above normal.

The next question was one which would occur to any civil engineer. Was more calcium or less passing through the filtration plants and going out to sea? This was important because one way that the products of the parathyroid factories might raise calcium on the waterways was to prevent filtration into the sea. Experiments (also performed on dogs) by Isidor Greenwald of the Roosevelt Hospital in New York City, showed that the filtration plants were letting through most of the calcium that came to them. Great quantities were being washed out to sea. If one assumes that this land had its brilliant economists, and as a consequence imports were not increased, this new state of affairs would lead, over time, to a depletion of calcium in the depots.

In short, calcium would go from warehouses to waterways, through the filtration plants, and out into the sea. To metamorphose our land back into an organism receiving too much parathyroid extract, calcium would go from bones into the bloodstream, through the kidneys, and into the urine. Continued too long, this egress can have but one consequence: an undermining of the bones.

The investigators now knew what to expect from overactive parathyroid glands; they did not know that such overactivity ever occurred. This brings us to Charles Martell, the "investigatee."

7

Charles Martell, the Investigatee

In 732, at the battle of Poitiers, Charles Martell rescued the Christian world from the clutch of the Saracens. Our story is about another Charles Martell, another battle, another kind of rescue. During the late unpleasantness,* while Albert was fighting for Franz Joseph, his American counterpart, Charles Martell, was a navigating officer for transports in the service of Uncle Sam.

Our knowledge about him is less fragmentary than that about Albert. He was born in Somerville, Massachusetts. He entered the Massachusetts Nautical School in 1914 to be trained for the American Merchant Marine. He graduated in 1916 at the top of his class. He was cadet officer on the S.S. *New York* in March 1917, when she was mined, near Liverpool, with Admiral Sims and staff aboard. This occurred only a few hours after the United States entered the war. The end of the war found him navigating officer on the U.S. Army Transport *Shoshone*, which carried munitions and men to France. (His brother, Captain Judson Martell of E

---

* 1914-1918.

Company, 60th Infantry, was in a French grave; their mother had a Distinguished Service Cross in compensation.)

The Captain Martell who returned to Somerville after the armistice was a changed man. Some of the changes could be attributed to service in war. Some were the result of a rare and serious medical condition which would lead the Captain onto fields of battle more arduous than any he had experienced heretofore.

Armistice Day—November 11, 1918—can be used to mark the beginning of the struggle which was to add a second Charles Martell to the ranks of the immortals, a struggle which was to terminate fourteen years later on the twelve-hundredth anniversary of the battle of Poitiers. This struggle was not to be against marshaled Germans or ferocious Saracens, but against an inward, hidden enemy, elusive, never surrendering until isolated and imprisoned in a bottle. The field of battle was not to be glamorous.* The struggle was joined in one hospital ward and then another, in this operating room and then that, and this again. An unqualified victory was not to be. Rather, defeat in victory; or was it victory in defeat? But that is getting ahead of our story.

Captain Martell continued for a while the life of the sailor. At the time of the Armistice he had noted pains in his back. There were many good explanations for these: a strain while pulling rigging, a touch of rheumatism due to drenching, a fall on a pitching deck. The pains persisted and spread to his legs. In 1919, his fellow officers noticed that he was losing height and becoming pigeon-breasted. The Captain noted a few grains of gravel in his urine. Then,

* Are any?

while climbing a ladder, there was a slight twist and something collapsed in his knee. The Captain was confined to bed for the first time. A month later, when his ship came to port, he was taken to U.S. Marine Hospital Number 21 on Staten Island. X-rays were taken. Little was accomplished.

The next month found the Captain on the S.S. *Swanee*. As he stepped from the ship's gangway to a small launch, his other knee gave way. Something seemed fundamentally wrong with the structure of the Captain's underpinnings. Dwellers in the older residences in Baltimore tell of having the supporting beams of their houses suddenly, and for no discernible reason, give way. The problem is caused by organized communities of termites. These insects can eat out the inside of a beam and leave the exterior intact and apparently solid. One day, unexpectedly, the whole thing will collapse. So it was with the Captain; he stepped off the boat and his knee collapsed.

Hospital entry number two was at the Methodist Episcopal Hospital in New York City. A patch-up job was done on his knee: operation number one. Then followed, in rapid succession, more trips, now to the west coast of South America, now to the Orient. There was more consultation with doctors at this port and that, more disability, and more pain; more gravel was noticed at the end of urination.

Hospital entry number three was in June 1922, at the Government Hospital, Ancon, Canal Zone. The Captain had a fractured arm. Another repair job was done. Off he went again, but not for long. He tripped over a rug on his return to New York and broke his forearm. He came under the care of a physician in New York who diagnosed an "arthritis of the mixed perisynovial and hypertrophic type." He was advised to lead an "open-air life with hospital care."

It became clear after a two-year stay at the Marine Hospital on Staten Island that he had a disease which involved all of his bones. The criteria for the diagnosis of von Recklinghausen's disease were almost unknown in this country. The faulty diagnosis of osteomalacia was made. The Captain was sailing on uncharted seas. If he was to reach port safely, the seas had first to be charted.

This was no routine situation. It was a problem for an investigator, and the Captain, for the time being, was to become the investigatee. The Captain's fifth hospital entry landed him at Bellevue Hospital in New York City. The reader knows the diagnosis and what should be done about it; the reader knows the chart that the Captain needs; the reader knows that von Recklinghausen's disease exists. Captain Martell's welfare depended upon his physician learning these things. Fate dealt him a good card. Captain Martell entered the service of Dr. Eugene F. DuBois.

DuBois' background was strikingly different from that of Dr. Mandl. He came from a breed of investigators who took less interest in structure than in function. His academic grandfather was Karl von Voit of Amberg, Germany. That gentleman did not spend his nights at the microscope studying cells, learning to correlate a certain cell structure with a certain disease. Instead, he induced Maximillian II of Bavaria to build a respiratory chamber for him, a glorified glass box in which he could enclose an experimental subject. From the nitrogen eliminated in the urine and the carbon dioxide eliminated in the expired air, he could calculate the amounts of protein, fat, and carbohydrate being broken down in the body. He attracted brilliant students. The whole science of nutrition and energy-exchange was developed by those who had been students of Karl von Voit. One of the greatest of these was Professor Graham Luck of Cornell University.

DuBois was a pupil of Graham Luck. His name has become familiar to physicians because of the DuBois chart. This has no direct bearing upon Captain Martell's voyage on uncharted seas. Yet, inasmuch as the Captain's life was for the time being in the hands of Dr. DuBois, any insight into his qualifications for this responsibility is of interest. What, then, is the DuBois chart?

The general law had been worked out that the energy expended by a normal person under certain standard conditions is proportional, not to the weight, not to the height, but to the body surface. The same is true of animals. In one famous experiment, a horse weighing 441 kilograms was compared with a rabbit weighing 2.3 kilograms. The horse expended 11.3 calories per kilogram, while the rabbit expended 75.1. Calculated on the basis of surface area, however, the horse expended 948 calories per square meter and the rabbit expended 917. This energy exchange, in relation to the surface area of the body and under standard conditions, is the mysterious concept of "basal metabolism." To determine the basal metabolic rate, then, the area of body surface must first be calculated. But how can this be done? Such was one of the many problems worked upon, and solved, by DuBois.

With his cousin Delafield DuBois, an electrical engineer, the solution was derived in the following manner. The patient to be studied was dressed in tightly fitting underwear, thin socks, and cotton gloves, with a section of the leg of a knitted undersuit pulled over the head and neck. Upon this groundwork were pasted strips of manila paper, until a flexible but inelastic mold of the body was completed. This mold was then removed by curved bandage-scissors, cutting the mold into pieces that were small enough to lie flat. These pieces were then coated with paraffin and placed in a large printing frame over sheets of photographic paper. Prints were made in the sun. The unexposed paper under the pieces of the mold were cut out and weighed. It was then an easy matter to determine the surface area of the body.*

The surface areas of tall fat people were compared with those of short thin people. Measurements from people of all different shapes and sizes allowed a chart to be constructed from which the surface area of any given person could be derived if the height and weight are known. This is the DuBois chart. As a result, one does not have to buy cotton tights when one wishes to have one's basal metabolism investigated. One still has to pay $5 ($10 in New York).†

The fate of the Captain, as he lay in a ward in Bellevue Hospital, slowly excreting his skeleton into his urine, was in the hands of this investigator. DuBois first did a careful history and physical examination. (In a hospital, one "does" a history.) No important facts were elicited which the reader does not already know. X-rays were taken. These showed that all bones were very transparent, lacking in mineral elements. There was evidence of multiple fractures. The usual laboratory tests added nothing.

What conclusions did DuBois draw? First, he realized that the disease, whatever it was, was entirely unknown to him. It was just as well, for to have known its name and not its treatment would have been of little value. He was confronted with a man of great vigor who was being diminished

---

* Pause inserted so that the reader can catch up on the various steps.

† The extra charge is not a royalty for Dr. DuBois, but just New York.

by a generalized crippling bone disease about which he, Du-Bois, knew almost nothing. "To know nothing about a disease" from the doctor's point of view, even in the best of families, is not unusual; from the patient's point of view, worse things can happen.

Consider, for comparison, diseases about which almost everything is known, including the fact that they are always fatal. One might say, "Where there is life and no diagnosis, there is hope." The public believes all too often that in this thirty-third year of the twentieth century a reputable doctor knows all about the majority of problems with which he is confronted. He doesn't. Every hospital ward has its quota of patients suffering from conditions which are understood imperfectly, if at all.

Hope for these people depends upon careful investigation. As the layman puts it: "He must be experimented upon." All sorts of orifices must be explored by various specialists; body fluids must be withdrawn and an ever-increasing number of chemical determinations made upon them. A menagerie of mice and guinea pigs must receive injections of these body fluids, and changes in the recipient animals must be recorded precisely. An abnormal finding may turn up anywhere in this chain of observations. It must be checked and double-checked. Every lead must be run down.

Any unusual finding must be compared with other similar findings described in publications from Paris, Vienna, Tokyo, Moscow, Sydney, or wherever. You say that this last step would be impossible. In fact, it is the easiest of all. How it is done will become clear when the *Index Medicus* is discussed.

This kind of investigation requires machinery: laboratories, animal farms, technicians, dietitians, chemists, physicists, etc. Most of all, however, it requires a special kind of doctor. These doctors must have special training. They must have what is termed "the investigative point of view." They must have worked at the advancing frontiers of knowledge to become familiar with the techniques of scientific and experimental study. It does not matter what they study, be it the number of square feet of skin covering a human being or the cause of Captain Martell's bone fractures; the scientific process is the same for all questions. They must have time to devote to a problem.

The busy general practitioner is in no position to give up practice for six months so that he can dedicate his attention to the disorder of one patient. Such singlemindedness, however, is necessary for the advancement of science. This means that if investigation is to flourish, farsighted individuals and institutions will have to continue to endow this investigative breed of doctor for the good of the flock. In any given community, unless a genuine effort is being made to extend the frontiers of medical knowledge, practice lags far behind the actual frontier. This, of course, is especially true for those frontiers advancing most rapidly, *e.g.*, the study of glands.

It will be worthwhile, perhaps, to pause a moment and examine in more detail one of these centers of medical activity. I say "center" of activity because the days of dispersed medical practice, the days of the country practitioner, have vanished. Parenthetically, all doctors, when introduced to strangers, are tired of being greeted with, "Oh, you're a doctor. I always thought I would like to be a doctor, but I never could stand the smell of ether. I do think we should have a return to the days of the good old family doctor. Everybody wants to be a specialist now, etc, etc." Whether we like it or not, the family practitioner, in the old sense, will disappear as surely as the cavalry charge. Medical practice will group itself more and more around centers.

Several critical components make up a medical center. In the first place, there is the physical equipment: wards, laboratories, apothecary shops, outpatient departments, and the rest. Then, there must be nurses, dietitians, technicians, social service workers, and stenographers. The doctors are of two types: "endowed" full-time men who depend chiefly upon a salary provided by the institution, and "practicing" doctors who depend chiefly upon fees provided by their patients. The full-time doctors, by design, have sufficient time to attack the special problems presented by unusual or unique patients. They are trying constantly (or should be) to push forward the frontier of medical knowledge. The large majority of them, of course, make no world-startling shove. A surprising number, nevertheless, contribute a slight push in some direction.

The important effect of this arrangement, however, is that those would-be Pasteurs, working on their problems, know their frontiers and keep the whole community of doctors with whom they are in contact current and up to date. The investigators work at public expense; the healers profit from the investigators; the public profits from the up-to-dateness of the healers. It all costs money, but it is the key to high-quality medicine. In the narrative of the voyage of Captain Martell, the reader can see this expensive machinery in operation and can judge for himself whether or not he considers it worth the cost.

When investigator DuBois met investigatee Martell, the logical result was investigation. But where to begin? The reader, having been presented with all the pertinent facts, doubtless is thinking that the answer is easy. All big advances, however, sound simple in the telling. Remember that the Albert/Mandl drama was still in progress. Remember that the association of a generalized bone disease with a parathyroid tumor was as good as unknown this side of the Atlantic. Remember that the best-known bone diseases of the time were due either to an inadequate intake of the building blocks for bone construction or to infections or tumors involving bones. Who would be so unconventional as to suspect that the little parathyroid factories could play a part?

But if DuBois did not know about the parathyroid tumors in von Recklinghausen's disease, he did know about Collip's work; he did know that products of the parathyroid factories played an important role in the transport of calcium on the inland waterways; he did know a measuring stick which could be applied for determining the activity of these factories. He gained immortality by applying this measuring stick in the case of Captain Martell.

A sample of blood taken from Captain Martell's arm contained more calcium than normally should be there! If the measuring stick was reliable, this meant just one thing. DuBois immediately took advantage of his lead. He prepared an experiment. He quantified all the calcium that the Captain ingested and all that he excreted. He found more going out than coming in. This paralleled the findings in Greenwald's dogs that had received an overabundance of Collip's bottled parathyroid products. It also agreed, as will appear later, with data which were being obtained at the Massachusetts General Hospital in Boston. The tentative diagnosis of an overproduction of parathyroid products (hyperparathyroidism) was made for the first time in this country; for the second time in the world.

Thus, the American school reached the same conclusion with Captain Martell that the Viennese school had reached with Albert. The American school lost the race by only a few months. The two routes had been entirely different. The physiochemical approach contrasted with the pathological approach. In the one case the disease had been put together; in the other it had been pulled apart.

8

More Digressions

Medicine is serious business. One cannot jump to conclusions. Hundreds of measurements of calcium were made on food, excretions, and blood, before a surgeon was called and told, "Look here, we believe Captain Martell has parathyroid glands which are putting out too much hormone into his bloodstream; what can you do about removing part of his glands?" To understand the confirming evidence that preceded this act is a story in itself. For this, we must leave the Captain a short while and travel to Boston to examine some data being collected at the Massachusetts General Hospital.

This quest will take us to Ward 4 in the historic Bulfinch Building. The Bulfinch had its cornerstone laid in 1818, its first patient in 1821, and its proverbial visit from General Lafayette in 1825. Among the historic notes relating to this building, one finds under October 16, 1846, the following: "Sulfuric ether was first used for the prevention of pain in a patient undergoing a serious operation at the Massachusetts General Hospital. This application was made by Mr. W.T.G. Morton. The experiment was a success." The Captain was to spend several October 16ths, "ether days," in this same building; on more than one occasion he was to receive the same anesthetic. A day was to come when the name of Captain Charles Martell would be better known through those gray walls of Chelmsford granite than that of Morton, not to mention that of Gilbert Abbott, the patient in the drama of 1846. Abbott was an investigatee; the Captain was an investigatee and, at the same time, an investigator.

But what was Ward 4? How did it differ from other wards, Ward 16 or Ward 31 for example? Every doctor who has worked in a general hospital has experienced something that is difficult to convey to the non-medical public: each hospital ward has a personality of its own. A home that has been lived in for several generations, where births, deaths, and marriages have taken place, where happy and sad moments have been passed, engenders something which endears it to the family. Just so, a ward, where the doctor is constantly struggling against the inevitable, where there is a sprinkling of dramatic successes and lighter moments among the tragedies, where a lifetime of incidents is crowded into a few weeks, assumes a unique personality and gains a place of affection in the hearts of those whose business it is to work there.

It would not be difficult to dissect the personality of a ward into its component parts. There are three main streams of influence; one is derived from the attending physicians, one from the nurses, and one from the patients. Consider Ward 31. Ward 31 is the male ward of the West Medical Service of the Massachusetts General Hospital. Many of its present-day traditions and ways of doing things can be traced back to Dr. William H. Smith and, before him, to Dr. Frederick C. Shattuck.

Strong personalities leave their mark. For instance, the

following story about Dr. Shattuck was told by Dr. Smith on his ward rounds one day. (In this manner, by the way, the strong personality of Dr. Shattuck, not to mention a little of the art of medicine, was transmitted to a younger generation.) Making rounds with students and house staff, Dr. Shattuck came to the bed of a neurotic patient who had vomited everything she had eaten since her admission to the hospital. The intern explained this to Dr. Shattuck. He said nothing and passed on to the next patient. Next morning, same story. Still he said nothing, and passed on. On the third morning the intern, with a worried expression, announced again that the patient had been unable to hold anything down. The eyes of the patient were fastened on Dr. Shattuck in a challenging sort of way that seemed to say, "Now do you believe this is serious?" He turned quietly to the nurse and ordered a stomach tube, two raw eggs, and a glass of milk. Dr. Shattuck then passed the tube down the patient's esophagus, into her stomach, and poured into it the glass of milk and the two raw eggs. Pulling out the tube, he said, "Now, I dare you to vomit." She didn't.

Nurses similarly contribute tremendously to the spirit, tradition, and personality of a ward. This applies especially to the head nurse, others being too transient and subordinate to leave much of a mark. The feeling that a doctor has for a ward can be influenced considerably by the type of head nurse. If she is pretty, that is* with a ready smile, a sense of humor, and a positive outlook on life, the ward will have a warmth that attracts physicians, patients, and families. Doctors like to work there; patients like to be there. These wards handle desperate illness well. These head

* The editor's reconstruction of the text begins here.

nurses tie their sense of success to outcome: did the patient live or die; was death gentle or hard; can the family cope? Most of these nurses are young; they leave nursing before they are old. The collective trauma of the inevitable loss upon loss proves too much. Most find new and less costly outlets for their humanity in home and family.

Then there is the "executive." These head nurses, no matter how attractive or cordial, generate a chill that permeates the fabric of the ward through and through. They tie their success to "clean management." These wards are judgmental places that subsist on documentation, sign-off sheets, and incident reports. Best not to make a mistake here. These are not good wards for difficult problems. Doctors spend as little time here as possible; the patients are usually "well." Wards like this are best suited for the executive physical and the V.I.P. admission.

Finally, there is the "staff sergeant." These nurses are the survivors. They have learned, or knew in the beginning, to tie their success to the quality of nursing care, not to outcome. They are affected by tragedy only insofar as the nursing process is flawed. If it is not, which is the usual case, the trauma is sustained and the next patient enrolled. These head nurses understand the goals of the ward and dedicate themselves, in collaboration with the doctors, to achieving them. This kind of head nurse is ideally suited to manage a research ward, where specimens must be collected in the correct way, at the correct time, in the correct sequence, under the correct conditions, over the correct duration.

The research ward,* a product of the mind of a doctor of the genus *investigator*, has made a distinct contribution to

* The author's words resume here.

medicine. The need for such a ward can never be realized by anybody who has not attempted to collect a twenty-four-hour specimen of urine from a patient on a general ward.

How is it done? There is an order book where the request is written in explicit English. The request is underlined boldly. The head nurse, the patient, the orderly, and possibly the patient in the adjoining bed, are consulted in an attempt to interest them in the problem. An effort is made to impress upon them the notion that the success of the patient's stay in the hospital depends upon getting an accurate collection. They are urged to remind the patient that the whole twenty-four-hour specimen must be saved for special analysis.

Does this succeed? No. On the other hand, try to interest these same people in seeing to it that the patient has a gargle, that he is sent to the x-ray department, that he blows air into bottles to exercise his lungs, and success is assured. But the amount of calcium in the urine in twenty-four hours, why, anybody can see that this has little to do with the hip fracture. The head nurse forgets to tell the night nurse; the night nurse forgets to tell the night orderly; the night orderly takes the specimen to the wrong laboratory; the technician in the wrong laboratory does the wrong test on the right sample. The net result is less than zero. Nothing is accomplished and everyone is upset. Complicate the problem by trying to have the patient eat an exact diet, no more and no less, and collect all excreta for several months without a slip. It cannot be done.

The solution is a research ward. The solution is Ward 4. When Doctor James H. Means became head of the medical service at the Massachusetts General Hospital, he was aware of these difficulties. He realized that better investigation required a small ward connected to a laboratory rather than more laboratories connected to general hospital wards. Ward 4 was born. It consisted of five two-bed rooms, a special kitchen, a trained dietitian, a carefully selected head nurse, and a large laboratory. Ward 4 was a paradise for investigation. Head nurses on this ward (there were only three) were known to have contemplated giving up nursing if a single urine specimen was lost. Scarcely a mouthful of food eaten on Ward 4 during the whole ten years of its existence had not been weighed to several decimal places and its exact chemical content determined. Everybody understood what it was all about; all cooperated; accurate data were collected; advances were made.

And now for the investigatees. These patients differed from the usual run of hospital patients. Many of them had disorders of internal secretion. It was not an unusual sight to see the green terrace in front of Ward 4 looking like a sideshow. A grotesque giant might be playing ball with a midget while the fat lady looked on. All these "misbuilts" of society lived on Ward 4 as one happy family. Some of the investigations lasted months; some lasted years.

Certain patients stand out in memory more clearly than others. There was one young girl, Katherine Lucy, whose parathyroid factories had been removed in another hospital when her overactive thyroid gland had been surgically excised. The calcium in her inland waterways was very low. Her telegraphic system was in a constant state of overactivity. She didn't play with the others because any exertion brought on painful muscle spasms. She sat quietly in her room. She ate the same diet for months at a time so that the measurements that were made on her urine and blood would be reliable. She had blood drawn from the vein in her arm almost every day. She taught the profession some very important things about the problems associated with her condition. In the end, she died during the removal of an infected tooth.

Every doctor knows that there is no justice. The finest characters die, others get well. What she taught her physicians would prove more valuable for the treatment of others than for herself. This was true for most of the investigatees.

Some patients began to consider it a fairly pleasant career to be a patient on Ward 4. One elderly gentleman, Ben Wiener, had an interesting condition that allowed him to spend eight months a year eating Ward 4 diets. When he learned that Dr. Walter Bauer had completed the studies on his particular condition and was beginning a study of rheumatism, he turned up one day with a limp.

So much for the background of Ward 4. Let us return to the data which were of so much interest to Dr. DuBois in his attempt to find the cause of Captain Martell's illness. This leads us to Dr. Joseph C. Aub, to lead poisoning, and to patients with hereditary deafness due to otosclerosis. It takes us to another great principle in medical investigation: a truth learned about one thing often sheds light on something apparently quite different. What possible connection could there be between Captain Martell, lead poisoning, and people with a hereditary form of deafness? There proved to be a very distinct one.

Dr. Aub is an academic brother of Dr. DuBois. Both were the academic sons of Graham Luck and, therefore, grandsons of Karl von Voit. The rubber industry wished to learn more about lead poisoning and was willing to finance some investigations to minimize, if possible, this serious and widespread hazard to its workers. Aub was chosen.

Ward 4 was about to open. Patients with lead poisoning were quickly gathered together, and the game began.

The first objective was to understand what happened to lead after it entered the body. It soon became apparent that it mimicked calcium in almost every respect. Wherever calcium was, lead was. When large amounts of calcium were excreted in the urine, the same was true for lead. They were both stored in the same warehouses (bones). When calcium was being leached from the bones and transported in large amounts in the blood, so was lead. The important truth that emerged after hundreds of laborious analyses was this: to make lead do what you want, make calcium do the same thing. What was wanted in this case was to increase the excretion of calcium and, thereby, to increase the excretion of lead. How could this be achieved? Is calcium excretion increased if calcium in the diet is increased? Is calcium excretion increased if the acid in the diet is increased?

The answers to these questions were ground out on Ward 4. Dozens of food articles were analyzed for their calcium content and a well-balanced diet of known calcium content was developed. Patients ate this diet for weeks. Urine and feces were collected for three days at a time. The calcium contents of the excreta were analyzed. Nineteen normal subjects each contributed fifty-three three-day collections. At the conclusion of the study, Dr. Aub and his colleagues felt confident that they knew how much calcium normal subjects, under "standard" conditions, excreted in urine and feces. In short, they knew the daily net loss of calcium from the body. They were now in a position to study the effects of various agents and manipulations on calcium excretion.

Collip's bottled parathyroid substance became available at about this time. All investigators were talking about it. Carefully conducted human experiments had not yet been done. It was predicted, however, that "parathormone" would have a powerful effect on calcium excretion. What affected calcium should affect lead. Would this general law still hold? Studies were set in motion to see how parathyroid substance altered the excretion of calcium and lead from individuals on the standard diet. The truths in connection with animals, established by Collip and Greenwald, were confirmed in man.

When bottled parathyroid substance was injected in excess, the amount of calcium on the inland waterways was high, and increased amounts were going out through the filtration plants to the sea. The same was true for lead. An extremely efficient method had been found for "deleading" a human being. Efficient, yes, but not too pleasant. The level of lead in the inland waterways leading to the brain became so high that changes in mentation were often produced. There can be too much of a good thing. But the parathyroid substance in moderate amounts proved a success in treating lead poisoning.

If something helps one thing in medicine, somebody will soon realize that it may help something else. It usually doesn't, but in proving that it doesn't, new facts are learned and progress muddles along. Moreover, the less known about a disease, the more hopeful seems any new suggested form of therapy. Practically nothing was known about otosclerosis except that it was a hereditary form of deafness coming on at puberty and made worse by pregnancy or lactation. So little was known about it that somebody with the disease left a large sum of money to be devoted to its study. This was a foolish thing to do. It would have been better to leave the money to some likely young investigator to use as he saw fit. Knowledge so gained is often found useful where least expected as, for example, in otosclerosis. If this is a prejudiced view, it doesn't matter: the money was left. And there it sat. People wanted money for this and money for that, but for the study of otosclerosis . . . there simply did not exist a single bird for that worm.

Sometimes, however, two objectives can be served at one time. Aub and associates ardently desired to give bottled parathyroid substance to additional human subjects so that more extensive data could be collected. This required money. The only money available, however, was for the study of otosclerosis. But wasn't it a well-known fact that pregnancy and lactation, both conditions that decrease the mother's calcium supply, increase the severity of otosclerosis? Perhaps calcium had something to do with the disorder. Was it possible that parathyroid substance might help otosclerotics? If not help them, at least do something to their hearing which would give a clue to the proper treatment?

Ward 4 was turned into a house party for young people with otosclerosis. They remained one month. They entered thoroughly into the spirit of things. They had almost daily hearing tests and repeated injections of bottled parathyroid substance. Calcium intake and output were carefully recorded. Hearing charts showed no change. The calcium data, however, proved very valuable. The money had been spent, science had advanced, and otosclerosis was still a mystery.

When Aub met with his former colleague, DuBois, these activities on Ward 4 were discussed. DuBois then described the Captain's case. What could be more revealing, it was agreed, than to give Captain Martell the same diet which had been used in all these studies and compare his

71

calcium values in the blood, urine, and feces with those of "normal" subjects receiving large amounts of bottled parathyroid substance?

Captain Martell bought a ticket to Boston and came to Ward 4 for his sixth hospital admission. He remained there six months. He immediately caught on to the rationale of what was in progress. He grew as impatient as anybody to know the result of each determination. His cheery person in bed or in a wheelchair on the terrace in front of Ward 4 became a hospital fixture. He talked with everybody. Betweentimes he read books, always about the sea. Sometimes he would just close his eyes and dream about the sea.

The data seemed conclusive. Either the Captain had too much parathyroid substance floating around in him, or he had something which was pretty similar. The calcium values for the Captain were almost identical with those of a normal person receiving one hundred units of bottled parathyroid product each day. The diagnosis of too much parathyroid substance (hyperparathyroidism) seemed justified, and surgery was advised. The Captain said "Sail on."

Behind him lay the gray Azores,
   Behind the Gates of Hercules;
Before him not the ghost of shores;
   Before him only shoreless seas.
The good mate said: "Now must we pray,
   For lo! the very stars are gone.
Brave Adm'r'l, speak; what shall I say?"
   "Why, say: 'Sail on! sail on! and on!'"

—*Joaquin Miller, "Columbus"*

9

The Uncharted Sea

A happy ending would have happened something like this: the Captain was prepared for operation; the region of the parathyroid glands was explored; a parathyroid gland the size of the end of a little finger (which would be twenty times the normal size) was found and removed; the gravel immediately disappeared from the Captain's urine; the bones gradually became more solid; Captain and Mrs. Martell lived happily ever afterward. But this would have been the story of a voyage on a charted sea; the Captain was sailing on uncharted waters.

Taking stock, it seemed reasonably certain from the chemical determinations that too much parathyroid substance was being produced. Although old stuff in Vienna, it was not known in Boston at the time that, in all likelihood, one could expect to find a tumor of one parathyroid gland. It seemed to those in charge of Captain Martell equally possible that almost normal-sized parathyroid glands might be producing the excess hormone. This situation is not infrequent with the thyroid gland.

The problem, therefore, did not seem so simple to Dr.

Edward P. Richardson, the surgeon who was consulted. He saw all too clearly that if there was a tumor, then the gland and tumor combined, although perhaps five times the size of a normal gland, might still be almost impossible to find amid all the structures in the neck. If there were no tumor, but merely normal-sized overfunctioning glands, then the problem would be that much more difficult. The reader must remember that even during an autopsy where there is little need to be careful of the many important vessels and nerves in the region, the parathyroid glands are rarely found. Surgeons who have performed hundreds of operations on the thyroid gland in the very region of the parathyroid bodies often state that they have seldom seen these tiny glands. The right kind of surgeon, however, recognizes these difficulties in advance, becomes more zealous as the difficulties increase, and leaves no stone unturned that might increase the chances for success. Edward Richardson, the son of the renowned New England surgeon Dr. Morris H. Richardson, was this kind of surgeon.

"Yes," he said, "I will operate in a few weeks time." Anatomy books were consulted. The parathyroid glands, it seemed, had a disagreeable way of lying in out-of-the-way places. Dr. Richardson spent hours over cadavers, finding the tiny glands and becoming familiar with their color and location. Finally, the day came when as many bridges had been crossed in advance as could be, and Dr. Richardson undertook the first operation of parathyroidectomy in this country, the second in the world.

The region of the parathyroid glands was carefully and thoroughly explored. Nothing that suggested a tumor was found. This was disappointing. Perhaps normal-sized glands were overfunctioning. A search for the tiny bodies was begun. This was a painstaking task. As every little suggestive body came into view, tissue was removed and handed over to a technician who froze it, cut it with a knife, and prepared and stained a microscopic slide. The slide was then examined by a pathologist to determine whether or not any parathyroid tissue was present. After five attempts, the answer was: yes, parathyroid tissue. One of the four factories had been removed. That was enough for one day. What effect would this have on the amount of calcium in the inland waterways, on the amount of calcium going through the filtration plants out to sea?

The Captain returned to Ward 4. More weighed diets, more collection of excretions, more anxious waiting for the completion of the tedious chemical determinations. Disappointment! There was no change. Another operation was performed; another factory was removed: another disappointment. The calcium content was still high in the inland waterways.

But there are two ways to kill a cat. Let the calcium be high in the inland waterways; let a large amount go through the filtration plants: what of it? Calcium is cheap. Tennis courts are made of it. To hell with the surgeons! Increase importation of calcium to meet the exports and, logically, the country should remain in calcium equilibrium!

This was tried. The Captain was given large amounts of calcium in his diet. Balance studies were repeated. The intake was greater than the output. Recovery seemed in the offing. The Captain became stronger.

His bones were stronger, yes, but he did not go back to sea. He sold insurance. To anyone who knew the Captain, that single fact meant just one thing: everything was not quiet on the Potomac. Or, rather, it was too quiet.

You will remember what happens when there is too little calcium in the inland waterways: the telegraph system is overactive. The opposite state of affairs exists when there is too much calcium: the telegraph system is sluggish; messages are slow in getting through; everything slows down; there is no zip.

The Captain just was not his old self. This was all the more trying, because by that time the Captain's story had caused other patients with moth-eaten bones to be found. Reports of complete cures of von Recklinghausen's disease were being published. After removal of the parathyroid tumor, these patients not only ceased to have bone symptoms, but stated that they had not felt so well in years. The Captain's bones improved, but he sold insurance.

A third operation in New York added nothing. Another trip to Ward 4 netted science some more observations, but netted the Captain nothing. The blood calcium content continued high and an abnormally large amount of calcium continued to filter out through the kidneys. The balance sheet, however, was positive because of the large calcium intake.

"The calcium continued to filter out through the kidneys," we said. It soon became clear that it did, and that it didn't. But this brings us back to Ward 4 and to a reconsideration of our consignment of the surgeons to hell.

While efforts on the Captain's behalf had seemingly reached a stalemate, this was not so for the work on Ward 4 in general. Other patients were found, tests were made, and tumors were removed. The complications of the disease began to be more clearly understood—one complication in particular. From the beginning it was noted that patients with this malady often had stones in the passages connecting the kidneys (filtration plants) with the outside world. These stones were deposits of calcium. This was not surprising. The urine was loaded with calcium, and calcium is a very insoluble substance. Suppose that our patient embarked on a long automobile trip in mixed company, forcing the urine to remain standing in these passages for a long time. Why shouldn't some of the excess calcium settle and coalesce into a stone? It should. It does. Furthermore, the stone, being composed mainly of calcium, could be seen by x-ray. Once seen, a surgeon would soon be after it. Once removed, another stone would be sure to follow. This rock mine for the unfortunate patient was often a gold mine for the fortunate surgeon.

Plumbing difficulties such as these are serious. The kidneys are necessary for life. A kidney can be put entirely out of commission by a stone downstream. Fortunately, there are two kidneys. One healthy one can carry the load. Too many stones, however, will eventually damage both kidneys. Inadequate filtration will result. Then, the game is up.

The Captain, by this time, had stones visible by x-ray. One kidney was out of commission, but the other seemed to be functioning adequately. An alarming fact, however, was becoming apparent. In this strange malady, stones do not form only downstream. Minute stones sometimes form in the kidneys themselves. The filters become clogged. This process slowly reduces the efficiency of the filters. It is one of those insidious conditions which can creep up so stealthily that, when first suspected, it is often too late. To make matters worse, a high intake of calcium, while beneficial for the bones, increases the amount of calcium passing through the kidneys. This increases the danger of developing this complication.

As his kidney problems became more and more apparent, the Captain was summoned again to Boston to see how matters stood. They didn't stand too well. One kidney was no longer working. The other was much impaired in function. The filters were becoming clogged. The Captain was between the devil and the deep blue sea. If he stopped taking calcium, his skeleton would vanish; if he continued, his kidneys would be destroyed. The treatment, which had seemed so logical, so simple, such a glowing example of modern medicine, had failed. A change had to be made. This brings us to the closing chapter. The surgeons are recalled from hell, and the Captain, face to face with the seriousness of the situation, takes the helm, no longer the investigatee, but now the fearless investigator.

Then, pale and worn, he kept his deck,
    And peered through darkness. Ah, that night
Of all dark nights! And then a speck—
    A light! A light; At last a light!
It grew, a starlit flag unfurled!
    It grew to be Time's burst of dawn.
He gained a world; he gave that world
    Its grandest lesson: "On! sail on!"

—*Joaquin Miller, "Columbus"*

10

Captain Martell, the Investigator

The removal of a parathyroid tumor had, by this time, become an occurrence of no great rarity. A case would come in with bone troubles; the measuring stick for the activity of the parathyroid glands would be applied. Overactivity often would be found. This would be talked over with the Captain. The day for the operation would be set and success would invariably result. The Captain would smile with a deep satisfaction. Others felt less satisfied. The Captain's tumor would be worth a hundred of these.

About once every month or so, the Captain persuaded the surgeons to make another attempt. His argument went like this: "We have studied this whole problem pretty well; our measurements are all similar to those of cases where the tumor has been found; the thing to do is to keep on trying until we get the thing in a bottle." Another attempt would be made: four more to be exact. All in vain. The old scar would be opened up, and every inch of tissue in the neck would be examined again, bit by bit, all the while avoiding a multitude of important structures. This would go on for hour after hour, finally stopping, followed by the bad news for the Captain. "Better luck next time," was always his cheerful reply.

But the surgeons were through. They were satisfied that there damn well was no tumor in the neck, measurements or no measurements. For all they knew, something was wrong with the measuring stick. "Nonsense," replied the Captain, "tumor there must be. Perhaps it is somewhere else."

Perhaps it was, but to understand how and where, we again must leave the Captain on Ward 3 (yes, Ward 4 had been closed because of the Depression) and this time journey to Sweden.

There, on March 5, 1927, a fifty-five-year-old woman, about whom a great deal has been written, entered the Seraphim Hospital. Her name has never been divulged, but we know that she was the youngest of eleven, eight of whom had died. She had three children, the youngest of which was an eighteen-year-old girl. The patient had gone through the "change of life" one year before. Thus far, not an unusual history. In the course of her menopause, she consulted a physician because of fatigue and back pain. Later, constipation and headache appeared. All physicians will agree that a woman of fifty-five with pain in the back, headaches, and constipation, even without a daughter of eighteen, can hardly be accused of suffering from unusual symptoms. Complete studies in the hospital failed to lead to a satisfactory diagnosis, and she was discharged with the diagnosis of neurosis.

A temporary improvement was followed by worsening. She began to lose weight. On September 15, 1929, she entered the Sabbatsberg Hospital. More studies, but still no diagnosis. An x-ray was taken of her chest. An unusual object, which did not belong there, was found. A patient without a diagnosis and a finding without an explanation. Two unknown facts should add up to something. Too late. She died on November 14, 1929. An autopsy was performed and the mystery was solved. The shadow in the chest was a parathyroid tumor arising from a misplaced parathyroid gland. Now we know why this patient had pain in the back.

The information which was revealed in that autopsy was precisely what was needed by the investigators at the Massachusetts General Hospital. Physicians in that hospital were desperate to know where a parathyroid tumor might be when it wasn't where it should be. But how was that knowledge to travel from Sabbatsberg to Boston? Except for the cumulative quarterly *Index Medicus*, published by the American Medical Association, it probably would not have. Four times a year, all articles from 1,302 scientific journals are cross-indexed according to subject matter and author. Thus, with very little effort, an investigator can cover every article in the world on a specific subject. In this instance, the subject was the parathyroid gland.

Dr. Hilding Bergstrand considered this case sufficiently interesting to be published. It was sent to the *Acta Medica Scandinavia* in March 1931, and appeared in the December 6, 1931 issue. It was indexed in the *Index Medicus* in the volume for October through December, 1931.

Whispered opinions that the Captain's tumor might be in his chest soon reached the Captain's ear. Another operation of any kind, particularly an operation on the chest, seemed inadvisable. By inadvisable, I mean inadvisable to everyone but the Captain.

He demanded an operation, partly as his last hope for recovery, but mostly to satisfy his scientific curiosity. He was determined not to die without first knowing whether or not the interpretation of the hundreds of measurements on blood, urine, and feces had been, in some way, incorrect. As a man with an instinct for self-preservation, he wanted that operation; as a scientist, he demanded it.

First, the stage had to be arranged. Mrs. Martell came up from Philadelphia for a visit. Instruments for splitting the sternal bone were designed and ordered. An excellent thoracic surgeon, Dr. E. D. Churchill, fortunately was available. He and Dr. Oliver Cope had done all the later operations on the Captain and had done the majority of the other parathyroid operations at the Massachusetts General Hospital. Dr. Churchill needed no introduction to the Captain. Thoracic surgery, with its special methods of keeping the lungs inflated while the chest is open, had been progressing by leaps and bounds and had reached a point where such an operation on the Captain seemed justified. The stage was set.

The drama was enacted on October 29, 1932; the anesthesia was given and the sternum was split. And there—I don't believe it! Yes! By God! Yes! There it was, cornered at last! Without mercy, be assured, was it dealt with. The sternum was sutured together again and the Captain returned to Ward 3. Mankind advanced another step forward in the struggle with disease.

Epilogue One

The boast of heraldry, the pomp of pow'r,
    And all that beauty, all that wealth e'er gave,
Awaits alike th' inevitable hour.
    The paths of glory lead but to the grave.

—Thomas Gray, "Elegy Written in a Country Churchyard"

One month later, the Captain was beginning to stand again. A bit unsteady, to be sure, but with bones considerably improved. Then, the very next day, the Captain stopped passing water. A stone had dammed up the outlet of the remaining kidney. An emergency operation was performed. The Captain did not rally from this as he should. The situation, ironically, was complicated by there being too little parathyroid tissue. He died; or was it just that his job was over? Not quite over. He had arranged, long before, that a thorough autopsy be done so that all the scientific data about him that had been collected over the years would be of the greatest possible value. A mariner, a scientist, and a gentleman. He died that others might live.

Epilogue Two

Little Jack Horner sat in a corner,
 Eating his Christmas pie;
He put in his thumb,
 And pulled out a plum,
And said, "What a good boy am I."

Margaret Dorothy Racicot, a married woman from Worcester, Massachusetts, entered the Massachusetts General
Hospital on November 3, 1932, five days before the parathyroid tumor was finally found and removed from Captain
Martell. Her story is of interest. It had started three years
before. She first noticed a dull aching in her arms, knees,
and lower legs. The feeling would last for one to two weeks
and then suddenly cease. "Plasters" and massage were used
to no avail. Several months later, while she was walking
down a flight of stairs, her left knee gave way beneath her.
She nursed a swollen knee for some weeks. The left hip then
began to ache. Other regions were heard from; pain became
incessant. Finally, a doctor was consulted! She learned that

she had rheumatism. Medicine was prescribed, but yielded no relief.

Then something happened that made it quite necessary for Mrs. Racicot to go to a hospital. Was it that she was unable to cook, unable to dress herself, unable to walk? No: she was unable to get into an automobile. One of the essentials of life had been interfered with and to the hospital she went, a broken-down machine in a machine age. X-ray studies were performed. Consultants were called in. Blood studies were made. Her neck was operated upon. A small tumor was removed. Would she get better? Alas! Microscopic examination showed that the tumor was not a parathyroid tumor but a small tumor of the thyroid gland, a thing of no importance. The wrong factory had been removed. The factory sought was apparently well camouflaged.

Matters did not improve; they became worse. There were more goings and comings to the hospital. A second operation was performed. The whole region was looked over; pieces of tissue were snipped off here and there; the microscopic examination failed to show parathyroid tissue. Where have we heard a similar story before? Mrs. Racicot was on crutches by this time. A course of x-ray treatment to destroy the factory by roentgen ray was tried. There was no relief. She was then sent to the Massachusetts General Hospital where, by this time, there had been four successful operations, even though the doctors there were still stymied by Captain Martell's case.

What arrived? A bedridden woman with extremely decalcified bones, multiple fractures of the bones of the pelvis, a fractured collarbone, several fractured ribs, cysts of the jaw, teeth sticking out in all directions, and very large amounts of calcium in her blood. Her kidneys still had good function. She had the disease without question; the possibility of cure was there if the treacherous rascal could be found.

Dr. Cope operated just seven days after the Martell drama. A careful search of the thyroid region was made. The going was slow because of scars from the previous operations. Nothing was found. The Worcester surgeons apparently had not overlooked anything. There was one more chance. Could lightning strike twice in the same spot in the same week? Dr. Cope worked a finger down under the sternum to the same location where the Captain's tumor had been hidden. The aorta could be felt pulsating. That was as it should be. "I think I feel. . . ." In the amphitheater several hearts stood still. "Yes, I am sure there is a tumor there." After a few long minutes, another finger had been worked down; the tumor had been freed and up into the neck it came! Mrs. Racicot lived happily ever after and soon had no difficulty in getting into automobiles.

Charles Martell had not lived in vain; before he died he knew that the solution of his problem had been the solution of Mrs. Racicot's. Time marches on!

Epilogue Three

How,* in fact, did we arrive at the solution for Mrs. Racicot's problem? The process begins with the idea that a question, correctly formulated, can be answered by a combination of correct thinking and experiment. We call this combination the scientific method. This method for finding truth was not revealed fully formed, but was developed over almost the whole of recorded history. The Pythagoreans, in the sixth century B.C., gave it first breath. They found that much of the world could be conceptualized in terms of numbers, and that these numbers, dealt with in the abstract, could lead to new and often startling insights.

Aristotle, 400 years later, formalized rules for associating ideas, the rules of logic. These rules, applied to ideas expressed in numbers, form the intellectual core of the scientific method. In parallel, Aristotle developed the system of observation and classification that provided the structure of modern biology and medicine. Scholars continued to work almost exclusively with the Aristotelian contributions for the

* The editor's reconstruction of the text begins here.

next 2000 years. These scholars applied the rules of logic to all manner of dogma. They excelled at testing consistency; they did not excel at testing the "truth" of assumptions.

Then, in 1589, Galileo did an experiment, dropping two dissimilar weights from the top of the tower of Pisa. In an instant, it became clear that at least one of the assumptions was wrong. The notion of experiment caught on fast. Its greatest champion was Francis Bacon, who formulated new ways of doing science which included experiment and an innovative way of deciding what to experiment on: the method of inductive thinking. Ideas for experiments began popping up everywhere.

For Mrs. Racicot, however, we need to follow the thread into the emerging science of physiology and medicine. The thread leads first to Magendie, who insisted upon minimizing* speculation and founding science on measurements; then to Bernard, Pavlov, Bayliss, and Starling for establishing the principle of an internal secretion; to Loeb for studying the effect of changing the amount of calcium in the environment of cells; to Erdheim for noting the changes in the teeth of rats without parathyroid glands; to MacCallum for developing a measuring stick for parathyroid activity; to Collip for getting the active principle out of animal parathyroid glands with the use of that measuring stick; to Collip and Greenwald for studying the effect of excessive doses of bottled parathyroid substance on dogs; to Aub and his associates for similar studies on humans in Ward 4; to DuBois for applying the measuring stick to a patient with a peculiar bone disease; to Mandl for first removing a parathyroid tumor in a patient with von Recklinghausen's

* The author's words resume here.

disease; to that small group of surgeons who have worked out the technique of the operation so that it is no longer like looking for a needle in a haystack; to the chemists who worked out the very accurate methods necessary for diagnosis; to the technicians who have painstakingly done all the analyses necessary for the clarification of the disease; and, last but not least, to the patients who, without exception, have submitted courageously to tedious experiments designed to solve first this point and then that. Of these, Captain Charles Martell stands foremost.

Epilogue to Epilogue Three

1935 has come and gone. The country is on the up; the New Deal is on the wane. In any case, prosperity seems to be returning, and Ward 4 is open again. The count stands at an even thirty patients who have had parathyroid tumors removed at the Massachusetts General Hospital.

Patient number twenty-eight was, and by the skin of his teeth still is, Eric Krause, a German glassblower of thirty-nine and the father of six children. Eric, for some time, had been losing weight and feeling badly. The diagnosis was not clear. He entered a nearby hospital and x-rays revealed that his bones were honeycombed. The measuring sticks were applied. It was hyperparathyroidism, and of a severe degree. The tumor was looked for and not found. One night Eric was a little delirious and jumped out of bed. Both legs snapped. This did not help matters. Furthermore, x-rays showed calcium deposits in the kidneys. The filters were clogging up. He didn't feel like eating. He couldn't move in bed because of his fractures; everything seemed discouraging; there were many complications; finally there was a long ambulance ride to the hospital.

What arrived? Seventy-one and one-half pounds of semi-conscious Eric with two broken legs and forty-two bedsores! He was all skin and bones and he had almost no bones and very little skin. What left 210 days later? A whole and hearty Eric, weighing 114 pounds, though still on crutches, to be sure, for a short time longer. What made the difference? The knowledge derived from twenty-seven other patients had been applied—that plus a mighty good nurse had done the trick.

And so on, *ad infinitum*.

Editor's Afterword

The life and work of Fuller Albright coincided with a shift of the centers of medical excellence from Europe to the United States. Albright was of the last generation of young physicians who felt it compulsory to make the continental tour. At the end of his life, it was young European physicians who felt it compulsory to have a fellowship in the United States. This remains so today. But just as societies and civilizations have their rise and fall, so do intellectual and scientific communities. Those of us who work in clinical science believe that we can sense the beginning of the "American Decline."

It is paradoxical that it should be so. We are experiencing a technological revolution that permits data acquisition and analysis at a heretofore undreamed of level. We are in the midst of a scientific renaissance that allows the study of disease on a new and fundamental plane. The science fiction of just a few years ago is today's reality, and there is no end in sight. Nonetheless, morale among the men and women that constitute the discipline of clinical investigation has never been lower. They leave in discouragement, and their numbers are not being restored.

The problem is one of guns *vs* butter. Our national budget exceeds one trillion dollars. One-third of this amount goes into "defense." Biomedical research receives six-tenths of one percent. This year, fewer than one in six new grant applications will be funded. The ratio for clinical studies is considerably less favorable. Most investigators derive their salary from this source, salary that provides food, shelter, and security for their families. It is a rare individual that is willing to stake this on a probability of less than fifteen percent, particularly when the alternatives are abundant and accessible. The practice of the medical sub-specialities, for example, has become less arduous and intellectually more satisfying, and remuneration is generous and sure. Taken together, these forces have decimated a generation of clinical scientists.

We hope for change. No society can allocate one-third of its national wealth for defense and long survive. If the threat is real, no amount of spending will hold the committed antagonist at bay for long. They will wait until the continued drain of resource so impoverishes our collective will and spirit that, enfeebled, we will fall. If the threat is not real, we will find ourselves with a powerful and efficient machine of war which defends a society weakened in human value and without scientific preeminence. It is Athens and Sparta at odds within one nation. Go to Athens and you find the core of western civilization. Go to Sparta and you may find a column or two in the grass. This must soon become apparent to us as a nation. Change will follow.

૨⪘   ૨⪘   ૨⪘

How science is done can be written down, like a recipe. The way it is done is learned by example. It is like a Bach fugue. The notes are the same for everybody. The way they are played, however, varies greatly. It is best to learn from an expert. We have two great names in American medicine. The first is William Osler. He was more physician than scientist. He left a great legacy in written material, anecdote, and biography. That legacy is as strong today as ever; American medicine lives in his image. The second great name is Fuller Albright. He was more scientist than physician. He left only his work. His "way" lived for a time in those that worked with him, but they are mostly gone now. The tradition is in jeopardy of being lost. Who will the next generation of clinical scientists look to for example and inspiration? I fear that the best of our generation will be beacons too distant to be seen clearly. These young people will be on uncharted waters and out of sight of land. They will need to set their course on a star. Fuller Albright is our star in clinical science. *Uncharted Seas* should brighten his presence for those who wish to follow. It has done so for me.

Kalmia Press is an imprint of JBK Publishing. *Uncharted Seas* has been designed by John Laursen at Press-22 and printed by Adprint Company during the summer of 1990. The type is Bookman, set by Irish Setter. The paper is acid-free Starwhite Vicksburg Archiva. Five hundred copies of the first edition have been bound in leather by Lincoln & Allen.